Praise for
Alton Carter's

The Boy Who Carried Bricks

"Carter's simple language and honest, matter-of-fact tone
create a narrative that is not only accessible and appealing,
but also an authentic account of what poverty, abuse,
and child welfare look like through the eyes of the young."
—Jewel Davis, *VOYA*

*****

"This book should be used in every school social studies class. A copy
should be in every counselor's office, church, and other youth organization
libraries in our country. This is a great book to give to any teen asking
the question, 'who am I and who do I want to be'—whether they be a child of
privilege or total social disadvantage and of every ethnic heritage . . .
The writing is good, and the story is true . . . All my grandsons and
granddaughters of grades sixth or seventh on up are getting this book
for Christmas. There is no better review from a bookseller than the
statement of, I am forking over my cash for this one to make sure
people I love can benefit from reading, *The Boy Who Carried Bricks*."
—*Larry Yoder, The Bookies, Denver, Colorado*

*****

"Although his memoir contains violence and mature themes—abuse,
foster care, poverty, crime—Alton Carter tells the story of his rough
childhood in a style that both enlightens and inspires. Older children will
see themselves and their classmates in Carter's portrayal of foster families,
teachers who stereotype, and peers who drag others into trouble.
This autobiography could guide at-risk children through tough
circumstances. It is at times heartbreaking but always hopeful."
—*ForeWord Reviews*

THE BOY
WHO
CARRIED
BRICKS

ALTON CARTER

THE ROADRUNNER PRESS
OKLAHOMA CITY

Published by The RoadRunner Press
Oklahoma City, Oklahoma
www.TheRoadRunnerPress.com

Cover Illustration & Design: Adam Headrick
Interior Illustrations: Janelda Lane

The RoadRunner Press is committed to publishing works of quality and integrity. The story, the experiences, and the words shared here are the author's alone. Some names have been changed out of respect for those who lived this story.

First edition hardcover, The RoadRunner Press, April 2015

OLD YA TRADE PAPER ISBN: 978-1-937054-19-9 | $14.00 U.S.
Also available in trade paper with a cover for younger YAs/middle-grades:
978-1-937054-36-6 | $12.99 U.S.

This book is also available for group sales by calling (405) 524-6205.

Publisher's Cataloging-In-Publication Data
(Prepared by The Donohue Group, Inc.)

Carter, Alton.
  The boy who carried bricks / Alton Carter. -- First edition.

    pages : illustrations ; cm

  Summary: Abandoned by his father, neglected by his mother, and shuttled between foster homes and a boys' ranch, a young African-American man refuses to succumb to the fate that the world says should be his. Told by the man who lived it.
  Interest age level: 012-018.
  Issued also as an ebook.
  ISBN: 978-1-937054-34-2

  1. Carter, Alton--Juvenile literature. 2. African American men--Biography--Juvenile literature. 3. African American youth--Social conditions--Juvenile literature. 4. Foster children--Juvenile literature. 5. Carter, Alton. 6. African Americans--Biography. 7. African Americans--Social conditions. 8. Foster children. 9. Autobiography. I. Title.

E185.97.C37 A3 2015
305.896073092 B   2014957122

10 9 8 7 6 5 4 3 2 1

For everyone, young and old, who has ever felt neglected, picked on, left out, or abused . . . and those who helped lighten the load

"Never give up, for that is just the place and time that the tide will turn."

— Harriet Beecher Stowe,
American author
and abolitionist
(1811-1896)

THE BOY WHO
CARRIED BRICKS

Introduction

My earliest memories of being a child are dark and terrible, memories I would not wish on another soul. Yet between the many horrific moments of my life, good happened, too. It usually came in the form of ordinary people, people who spared me a moment's kindness or a word of advice or a respite from the abuse and, in doing so, left me with a glimmer of hope.

But those who hurt me also made a difference in my life. They helped me decide at an early age that I wanted to be different than them. You may find it difficult to believe that a child can make such a decision, but I am here to tell you otherwise. Children see more than adults realize. Children feel more than adults know. Good teachers and good parents know this.

What differs from child to child is what the abused or neglected child does with the fleeting moments of hope that happen to come his or her way. Some children don't trust them. Others fear them. And more than a few squander them. There was something in me, however, that made me grasp hope, like a drowning swimmer grabs a rope.

Looking back, I now see hope sprinkled through my life like bread crumbs—and, just like a child in a fairy tale, it was up to me to be brave enough to follow the trail of crumbs home.

Yes, home. Not to the abusive home of my childhood but to the home of my dreams, the home I hoped to someday build for a family of my own.

You see, my dream was that I would one day become someone that no one in my family had ever been. My dream was that I would become a loving and stable father and husband, one who could provide my children with experiences and things I never had, not big things but the little things that so many take for granted.

I wanted my children to be able to look in the refrigerator and find food in it, not roaches. I wanted to rock my children to sleep at night. I wanted to be present for their first steps and the first time they rode a bike. I imagined Saturday mornings with all of us sprawled in front of the television in our pajamas watching cartoons as the smell of breakfast filled the room.

I wanted things for my wife that my mother never received from the many men in her life. I wanted my wife to know she would never need to be afraid of me, to fear that I would hit or harm her, with words or deeds.

I wanted to own a little house in which I could always turn on the light and control if it was hot or cold. I wanted to stay in a house for more than four months without being evicted.

Truth be told, I never dreamed about being rich or driving fancy cars or being famous. My wishes and dreams were simple because anything else would have been a fairy tale. But I know now that fairy tales are nothing more than dreams and hopes of how things could be—and what I needed, then and now, was not material things or glory but the things that are priceless: family, friends, respect, love.

I desperately wanted my nightmares to turn into fairy tales, so I dreamed of being different.

Early on, I realized that if I was going to be different, I needed to rely on people outside of my family. I knew I would need help because I had experienced enough bad to know I could not escape it alone. Getting out would take the help of others, so I dreamed of meeting people who would help me become what I wasn't. Call them angels or mentors or Good Samaritans, I learned to keep an eye out for them. And I listened to what they had to teach me.

Eventually, I came to believe that if I could survive what was happening to me, I would someday make a difference in the lives of others.

I am not suggesting my life, now or then, has been better or worse than anyone else's. Life has enough pain and suffering for us all. But there are almost 400,000 children in the United States living without permanent families in the foster care system—more than nine thousand in Oklahoma alone in any given year.

Many of them will never earn a high school diploma, and while seventy percent of all youth in foster care express a desire to attend college, only a mere six percent will finish even a two-year degree.

It doesn't have to be like that. And my life is proof of that. And that is why I share my story here, as a way of letting others facing difficulty know that their dreams can come true—even if you never knew your father, even if your mother abused you, even if you were shuttled between foster care most of your life.

I hope my story will encourage others to follow the bread crumbs . . . and to trust hope when it appears in their life.

This story is my life, told by me as I remember it.

Chapter 1
The Beginning

My birth certificate says Glendola Carter gave birth to me in Stillwater, Oklahoma, on September 27, 1970. My full name is Alton Odell Carter. The place on the birth certificate where my father's name should be is blank.

I don't remember my life as an infant, but by 1974 I was four years old and some things about my childhood were as clear as glass. My mother had five children by four different men. We all carried my mother's maiden name of Carter, so I can only assume she was never married to any of our dads. What I do know is none of the men stuck around to help take care of us, let alone give us their last name.

My brother Lavell was the oldest by two years, then me, and after me in quick succession came the twins, Kesha and Watell, and then the baby, Dejohn—four kids in four years, between shifts at fast food restaurants and various odd jobs. Mom left Lavell, five years old at the time, in charge of us while she worked.

Our life was far from ideal and then Mom started dating again. For whatever reason, she never kept a boyfriend long; the musical boyfriend chairs continued for about two years until she finally met a guy named Ray. I remember Ray as a guy of medium height with a medium-length Afro. He seemed to like Mom, and they got along pretty well. My brothers and sisters and I called him "Rabie."

For the most part, he treated us well too, considering we weren't his kids. He never did much with us, but he did spend a lot of time with Mom.

In 1975, after dating four months, Mom and Ray married. We moved from the university town of Stillwater about twenty-six miles northwest to Perry, Oklahoma, where Ray had grown up. We lived in a house on the east side of town near the railroad tracks. It was a little white, one bedroom, shotgun-style house, but we were proud of it. The little house sat on a corner lot with a huge oak tree in the front yard.

Train tracks ran behind the house, right beyond our big back-yard where we spent most of our time playing. When we weren't in the backyard, you could find us on the railroad tracks. We had contests to see who could walk the farthest on a single track. With our arms out to the side to help us balance, we walked the rail for what seemed like miles. When a train came, we would jump off to the side and watch it go by. The trains were loud, enormous, and miles long. I never understood how the engine in the back could push all those cars, much less push them so fast and so far.

If we weren't watching the trains go by, we were throwing rocks at the boxcars as they passed. Sometimes, people on the train would see us and yell, "Hey! You kids stop throwing rocks!" or "Go home before I tell your parents!" Their threats never scared us. The train could not stop fast enough to catch us, and even if it had, we were blocks away from our house, throwing rocks from someone else's backyard.

The railroad tracks provided us with all kinds of entertainment. One of our favorite pastimes was placing pennies on the rails of the track and letting trains smash the coins flat as they rolled over them. We loved the trains, but never thought about the danger we were in playing around them.

In all the times we played on the tracks, I don't remember my mother once coming to check on us. But I do recall the day my older brother came up with the idea of using rocks instead of pennies on them. We lined both rails with rocks for at least thirty or forty feet. Nothing terrible happened when the train hit the rocks—the rocks just exploded into bits and pieces, so it became a regular thing we did when we were bored.

We managed to avoid being caught for a long time, thanks to our mother's indifference and being blocks away from home, but our luck was not to last. One day Ray spotted us lining the rails with rocks on his way back from the store. I saw Ray first and told Lavell, and we ran home as fast as we could. When we arrived, Ray was standing on the back porch holding a black belt folded in half. It was obvious what was coming, and I was afraid—not of being whipped but because until now, no one had ever whipped us but Mom.

Lavell yelled for Mom as Ray grabbed me by my arm and began lashing me on my lower legs and bottom. I ran around in a circle screaming, as he held me with one hand and used the other to whip me. After a few good licks, Ray stopped and called for my brother. Lavell had retreated to the porch. He started towards Ray, and I saw Mom standing just inside the back door.

Why doesn't she do anything to stop him, I wondered. After all, we were not his kids. But as Ray whipped my brother just as he had whipped me, she never moved. I couldn't help but cry. I cried because my legs were covered with stinging welts. I cried because my brother was getting beaten. I cried because my mother did nothing to stop Ray. It all happened in slow motion. The belt swung back and forth, cutting through the air; it made a loud smack every time it struck my brother.

When Ray finished with my brother, he didn't say a word. He walked past my mom, who was still standing inside the back door, and into the house. After he had gone, I expected Mom to come out and console us, but she didn't. She closed the door, without a word, while my brother and I sat there in the backyard crying like babies. My brother didn't say it, but I know he felt betrayed by Mom just

6

like I did. *How could she stand there and watch Ray do that to us?* We stayed like that for quite a while. Eventually, we walked around to the front of the house. Ray found us there sitting in silence on the concrete porch. He paused with the front door still in his hand and gave us a good stare. Without a word, he walked to his blue pickup, got in, and drove off. As soon as he was out of sight, we ran into the house looking for Mom. We had questions. I wanted to know why she hadn't stepped in to save us from Ray. We found her in the back room, sitting on the bed, bent over with her hands covering her face. The same welts that covered our legs were rising up on her arms.

So that is why she didn't stop him, I thought.

Mom wiped the tears from her face and told us that we should do our best to not make Ray mad.

"Stay out of his way," she said.

"I hate Ray," Lavell said.

"No, no," Mom said, it was her fault. To hear her tell it, Ray was a good man, with a job, and he was going to be our dad and help her pay the bills. Neither Lavell nor I had a response to that.

The rest of that day was spent in silence, for no words could have soothed the mood. My younger siblings hadn't witnessed the beatings, but they knew something wasn't right and they kept quieter than normal.

We all went to bed that night with very few words. Mom laid us down to sleep on the living room floor and kissed us good night. I spent most of the night staring at the backdoor afraid to go to sleep, afraid Ray might return and finish what he had started.

Every time the blankets touched the swollen welts on my bottom and legs, I relived the beating Ray had given me. I looked over to see if Lavell, sleeping between Dejohn and Kesha, was faring any better but I found him staring at the ceiling. I wanted to talk to him but had no idea what to say, so I just stared at him until I fell asleep.

It was the first of many nights to come, nights we went to bed on the floor trying to sleep without moving because the blankets made the welts on our body sting. Yet there were good times as well.

8

Chapter 2
Nice Guy

No bad guy is bad 24/7. Even murderers take in the occasional ball game or movie. And Ray was no murderer. He could be nice, and he was helped by the fact that as children, we lived in the moment. Every day a child wakes up and thinks: today is the day it is all going to work out, today is the day my family becomes like the ones on *Leave it to Beaver* or *Mayberry R.F.D.*

My siblings and I were no different. We loved our mom, and we wanted to like Ray. We wanted him to be a good guy. And we took the smallest scrap of kindness or gesture of normalcy as a sign that it was possible.

I remember one day Ray came home late from work to find us playing in the backyard. He told everyone to come to the front porch because he had something for us. Once we had all gathered round, he walked to the back of his truck and pulled out two brand new bicycles and two of the coolest Big Wheels, I had ever seen. One of the bikes was for Lavell, and the other was for me. The two Big Wheels were for the twins. Dejohn was still just a baby and too young to ride anything.

Lavell's red bike had long, shiny handlebars with red grips, a banana seat, and chrome pedals. My bike was blue with regular handlebars, blue plastic grips, and black pedals. Kesha's Big Wheel was pink with red pinstripes and pink and white streamers bursting out of the handle grips. Watell's Big Wheel was blue and gold pinstripes with blue and white streamers.

It may be difficult to understand, but Ray's gift instantly made everything better, erasing the beatings from my mind, like an Etch A Sketch. *Things are going to be different now,* I thought. *Ray has changed.*

I could tell Ray's gifts for us had worked their magic on my mom, too. She sat on the front porch holding the baby, smiling and happier than I had ever seen her. We spent the whole day together like a normal family: Ray playing with us older kids, while Mom and Dejohn watched.

Ray even went so far as to set up an obstacle course for us. It started at the front porch, circled the tree in the middle of the front yard, and then followed the driveway into the street and down the block to the stop sign. Once we reached the stop sign, we were to turn around and head back up the street towards home. The return was the most exciting part of the course because Ray would run beside us into the driveway, like we were racing him.

Ray could have won every time, but he didn't. Instead, he let us get ahead for a while, and then he would catch up before letting us beat him to the tree. I beat Ray every time, but he made sure the race was close, and he acted like he was proud of me for winning. He would throw his hands up in the air and say he couldn't believe I had won again. Then he would tell me he was going to beat me the next time. We raced our new bikes and Big Wheels until it was dark, and we were no longer able to see where we were going.

It was one of the most normal nights of my young life. And I will always remember it. It wasn't about getting the bikes either, though that was nice. It was about feeling loved and like a normal family, even if for just one day.

Chapter 3
Fighting

The arguing and fighting had been going on all day but it had not escalated into physical violence yet.

By now, we had a routine. Anytime Ray and Mom started fighting, I would grab Watell and Kesha by the hand, and Lavell would get Dejohn, and we would go outside and sit on the front porch so we didn't have to witness the two of them go at it. Many a night the five of us sat out on the porch, trying to ignore the cussing and screaming on the other side of the door. Too often the sound of things being broken and furniture sliding around on the floor painted only too graphic a picture of what was happening inside.

One particular night we had been on the porch for hours, and the fighting had gotten so loud we couldn't ignore it anymore.

"I'm sorry . . . I'm sorry," our mother screamed. "Please stop. Please, Ray, please stop!"

Before she could scream again, Lavell ran to the front door, flung it open, and shouted at Ray: "Leave my mother alone!"

Instantly, Mom started begging, "No! No!" as Ray dropped my mother and started for Lavell.

Mom jumped up to put herself between Ray and Lavell, but before she could, Ray punched Mom in the face just under her right eye. She fell against the wall, slumping to the ground. Ray grabbed Lavell by the front of his shirt with one hand, drew back his other hand, and hit Lavell in the face. Lavell fell back on the four of us, knocking Watell and Dejohn off the front porch. Watell landed on his bottom in the dirt, while Dejohn tumbled head first onto the hard ground.

With her eye already swelling, my mom stood and let out a war cry. She balled up her fists and began beating Ray on his back. I ran at Ray and started hitting him anywhere I could hit him. Lavell picked himself up off the front porch and joined in the fight, kicking Ray in the legs over and over again. Ray ignored Lavell and me and focused all his attention on Mom. He grabbed her by a chunk of hair and began punching her in the stomach. With each punch I heard her body gasp. She finally broke free and ran to the bedroom in the back of the house, but she failed to lock the door. Ray followed her in, shouting, "You are going to get it now."

My siblings and I had followed Ray, but he shut and locked the door before we could enter. We couldn't see what was going on inside, but the sounds were all too familiar. There was no mistaking the sound of Ray's belt as it sliced through the air or the smacking sound as the belt struck Mom. Time and time again, the belt landed, and with each smack Mom let out the most gut-wrenching screams I had ever heard.

We hovered by the door for what seemed like forever. Helpless. Afraid. Hopeless. Finally the beating stopped, and we ran to the living room, for fear that he was coming for us next.

Huddled together in the living room with our arms wrapped around each other, all we could do was gawk when the bedroom door swung open and my mom came running toward us with a look of absolute fear in her eyes. You would have thought that she was being chased by the devil himself.

Ray appeared next and drew back his arm and threw something. With her arms wrapped around the five of us, Mom was shielding us from Ray when the object struck her head so hard that we all fell to the living room floor with Mom still holding us. In a pile, we hit the ground. I felt Mom let go of us as her body went limp.

I will never forget being down on the floor and looking over at her. Her eyes were open, but it looked as if she was dead. She was so still. Her eyes stared blankly at me, but it was as if she could not see me, like she was asleep with her eyes open.

Blood started pouring from the top of her head. My siblings and I began wailing, convinced Mom was dead.

At the end of the hallway, Ray still stood, no emotion on his face. He looked at Mom crumpled on the floor like a rag doll, not moving but bleeding profusely, and instead of calling 9-1-1, he faded back into the bedroom and shut the door.

Lavell tried to wake Mom. I heard Ray moving around in the bedroom and feared he would return to finish the job. He finally did return, but only to step over the six of us and walk out the door.

I heard him start his truck, before he drove off into the night. As the truck's headlights faded away, Mom began to moan. Lavell ran and grabbed some towels, pressing them to her head in an attempt to stop the bleeding.

Mom began to speak, but I couldn't hear what she was saying, so I leaned forward and put my ear closer to her mouth.

"I'm sorry, Alton. I will leave him tomorrow," she whispered.

With that, Lavell and I finished cleaning the blood from her head and helped Mom to her room and into bed. Then my brother and I went back and each took our place by our siblings on the floor, praying that Ray would not return.

Chapter 4
The Long Walk

The next morning Mom woke us very early. She was not at all herself, rushing around and telling Lavell and me to get dressed. She grabbed Dejohn who was still asleep and put clothes on him; then, she put clothes on the twins. Once we were all dressed, she put Dejohn and the twins in her beat-up, dark tan Buick that leaked oil and barely ran. She told Lavell and me to get in the back and that we were leaving.

In a panic, she ran back in the house one last time and grabbed a few small bags. When she returned, her hands were shaking, and she kept looking in the rearview mirror. Mom pointed the car east towards Stillwater, almost twenty-six miles away.

We had just crossed the railroad tracks and were headed out of town when the car started making a strange noise.

"No, no—not now!" Mom cried.

The car starting jerking and eventually came to a stop on the side of the road a few blocks from where we lived. Mom was frantic now, turning the key in the ignition and stomping on the gas pedal. The car only made a growling sound then fell silent.

"Are we going back?" I asked.

"No, we're not going back," she said. I could hear the resolve in her voice.

"But what about the car?" I said.

"We're going to start walking," she answered, "and someone will eventually stop and give us a ride."

Mom grabbed Dejohn and pulled the twins out of the car; Lavell and I followed. Leaving our bags behind, she put Dejohn on her hip, told the twins to hold hands, and started walking east out of town. None of us kids said a word.

By now the sun was rising up over the trees and shining in our faces. Mom kept looking over her shoulder in hopes that someone would pick us up before Ray discovered that we were gone.

We walked for several miles without resting, and it was obvious Mom was getting tired. With each minute it was also getting hotter and hotter, and soon we were all covered in sweat. We walked a few more miles before Mom was forced to take a break under a tree in front of a neat brick house.

We sat under the tree and watched car after car go by, but no one stopped or even asked if we needed help. After awhile, we heard a door open behind us. A middle-aged woman wearing a robe stepped onto the front porch.

"Are you okay?" the woman asked.

With tears in her eyes, Mom got up, grabbed Dejohn, and walked up the driveway to speak with the woman. They talked for a few minutes, and then went in the house. They were there for a short time when Mom returned, with the woman following her, carrying a glass and a pitcher of ice water.

The woman took Dejohn off Mom's hip, so she could pour us something to drink. The water was so good. I instantly felt better. We took turns until the glass was covered in dirty fingerprints, while Mom and the woman talked.

Mom said we were headed to Stillwater to get away from her abusive husband, but our car had broken down a mile or so back towards town. The woman said she wished she could give us a ride, but her husband was at work in their only car. She said if we stayed until her husband returned, she would give us a ride to Stillwater.

"Thank you," Mom said, "but we need to get out of town as soon as possible."

Our Good Samaritan offered to call the police, but Mom explained that would only make things worse. We finished off the water, and Mom thanked the woman for all she had done.

The woman handed Dejohn back to Mom, and we continued on foot out of town. I watched hope come and go as each car approached and passed us by. We would walk a few miles and then stop to rest wherever a tree could offer us some shade from the hot sun. Growing more and more thirsty, we walked until Mom was so weak she needed a break from carrying Dejohn.

Looking back, I have always suspected that twenty-six-mile walk from Perry to Stillwater planted the seed of resentment in my mother that would one day become a hatred of all mankind, including me.

The walk took all day—given that my mom had five children with her, four of them under the age of five including one she had to carry like a bag of flour, it is a miracle we made it at all. By the time we arrived in the neighborhood of my mom's friend Shirley, Mom had reached her boiling point.

Tired and grumpy, my siblings and I were doing our best to make sure Mom knew it. With every step we grew weaker, more tired, and more inclined to bicker. For the last few miles all we did was fight amongst ourselves. Mom was fed up and hollering at us to stop fighting, but we ignored her. Kesha and Watell were sick of holding hands and made sure to remind us of this over and over.

"How much further?" Lavell kept asking.

"I'm hungry," I whined.

Finally, Mom had had enough. She grabbed a switch from a small tree next to the sidewalk that led to Shirley's apartment and started whipping our legs, all the while shouting that she had heard enough out of us for one day.

Getting a whipping with a switch usually doesn't hurt as bad as a belt, but this night it felt like a bee sting every time she hit our legs.

As we walked, Mom kept swatting us with the switch until we were standing right at Shirley's front door.

With Dejohn still on her hip, she threw down the switch so she could ring the doorbell. That's when Mom noticed the blood. Her palm was covered in small puncture wounds. She looked from her hand to us.

"Oh my god," she cried.

Our legs were covered with blood. The switch she had used was from a thorn bush. Mom started crying.

"I am so sorry," she said, over and over.

While Mom was crying and apologizing, Shirley came to the front door and saw what Mom had done; I could see the embarrassment for Mom on her face. Mom tried to explain to Shirley what had happened, while Shirley hoisted Dejohn off Mom's hip and escorted us into her home. It was a very sad arrival.

Inside, Mom wiped the blood from our legs, Shirley ran some bathwater, and we were all put in the bathtub. Mom and Shirley left us to soak and retired to the living room to talk.

As Dejohn and the twins played in the water, Lavell and I listened to Mom tell Shirley about the violence we had endured over the past year at the hands of Ray. Mom explained she was so hurt because she had thought Ray was different from the other men who had let her down before. Shirley listened patiently as Mom told her story and cried.

After our bath, Shirley dressed us in oversized T-shirts and set us down at the coffee table in the middle of the living room. The twins, Lavell, and I gobbled sandwiches and chips, while Shirley fed Dejohn some Malt-O-Meal as Mom took a bath.

As we sat on the floor eating our first meal of the day, I could hear Mom crying once again behind the bathroom door. Shirley didn't say a word nor did she let her expression change. She just covered the couch with blankets and then tucked us in on the couch where we slept until morning. We stayed with Shirley for months before eventually moving into our own apartment.

Chapter 5
Getting By

From the end of 1975 to 1977, we relied on food stamps and government assistance to help us get by. We never stayed in a house or apartment for more than four to six months before getting evicted.

Mom stayed single for a while but became increasingly lonely and depressed. She was never quite the same after she left Ray. She began to take pills to help her cope with a life of gut-wrenching poverty, constant disappointment, and the endless struggle to raise five fatherless children.

I watched my once active, pretty Mom become lethargic and disconnected from the world around her. Our living conditions recalled a meth house more than a home—dirty clothes piles covered the floors, stacks of dirty dishes piled up on kitchen counters, and the dirty sink held as many roaches as dirty dishes.

Our cabinets held only a few canned goods while the refrigerator was almost always empty. As we grew older, we learned how to fend for ourselves because Mom was preoccupied with her prescription pills. Most days found us running around our dirty, roach-infested house with no electricity and Mom sleeping in her bedroom, shades drawn, hiding from reality. I might have still been able to empathize with Mom if that had been that; I was only a kid, but even I realized how difficult it was to raise five children alone with no money. But that wasn't the end of it.

Instead, my brothers and sister and I had to watch our mom come alive at night for strangers. She would get all dressed up and leave us home alone for hours—often not coming back until the next day. Sometimes when she did come home, she would bring some man home with her, but none of them ever stayed more than a day or two. I knew that was partly because she had five kids, but mostly because they were disgusted at how filthy our house was.

As time passed, Lavell, Watell, Kesha, Dejohn, and I changed, too. It was as if we reverted to our most base animal instincts, scavenging for food wherever we could find it, fighting for survival, oblivious to bugs or filth that would have shocked anyone else.

Little wonder. Our mother had basically left us to fend for ourselves, like wolf pups. We were hungry all the time. My siblings and I resorted to dumpster-diving behind local grocery stores for food. Lavell was forced to become our breadwinner, which turned him into a thief. He stole food from gas stations and supermarkets so we could eat.

Lavell and I did our best to take care of our younger siblings—but with no electricity that meant cold baths, with no money it meant dressing them in dirty clothes that didn't fit, and with no groceries it meant scrounging for whatever food we could find, wherever we could find it.

Eventually, our neglect caught up with Mom and forced the State Department of Human Services to get involved.

Chapter 6
Hot Bath

Looking back, it is difficult to believe that it all came down to a bath gone wrong. But life can change that fast.

Mom was sleeping off her daily dose of prescription pills, and Lavell and I had decided to give the twins and Dejohn a bath. I was six years old but by this time I was a pro at giving baths. As I had done so many times before, I ran lukewarm water in the tub; I put the twins at the back of the tub and Dejohn in front by the faucet.

Together, Lavell and I washed our siblings from head to toe. We checked their ears for roaches and then let them play in the tub for a while. It was just a normal night at the Carter house, when Kesha suddenly reached around Dejohn and turned on the hot water.

Scalding water rained on Dejohn. I jumped off the toilet seat and turned off the faucet, but it was too late. Already blisters the size of quarters had appeared on his left side. Dejohn just sat stunned. Not even a whimper.

Lavell pulled him out of the tub, and I ran to the bedroom to wake and tell Mom. She started screaming "My baby, my baby!" and ran to the bathroom. Lavell was holding Dejohn who still had yet to make a sound. The blisters were not so quiet. They had already grown angry-looking and merged into one giant blister that covered the entire left side of his body.

Screaming and crying, Mom grabbed Dejohn from Lavell's arms, wrapped him in towels, and told us all to get in the car. Mom drove as fast as her car would go, ignoring traffic lights and stops signs. We pulled into the Stillwater hospital parking lot, and Mom jumped out of the car with Dejohn in her arms and started running for the entrance. Inside, a nurse took my little brother from Mom's arms, back to an examination room. Lavell, the twins, and I sat in the waiting room for what seemed like hours, hoping Dejohn was okay. We were all so scared.

While we were waiting, a woman carrying a stack of folders appeared at the front desk and asked to see "Glendola Vick." The receptionist told her Ms. Vick was back in the exam room with the doctors. The woman with the folders then flashed her I.D. badge, and the two of them disappeared behind the double doors that led back to where my mom and Dejohn were.

I didn't recognize the woman and wondered why she was asking to see my mom. Minutes later the woman was standing in front of us in the waiting room. She kneeled and told us that she worked for the Department of Human Services, and needed to ask us some questions about what had happened to Dejohn.

She told us everything would be okay and she needed us to tell the truth. Lavell asked the woman where our mom was, and the lady said she was still with Dejohn, but we didn't need to wait for her. With that, she put her folders down on an end table, pulled out a notebook, and reached in her purse for a pen.

"Start from the beginning," she said.

Lavell and I took turns telling her how Dejohn came to be burned in the bathtub. She took notes, looking up at us from time to time. When I told her about waking Mom up, she asked me to repeat that part again. So I did, explaining that Mom had been sleeping while Lavell and I gave the twins and Dejohn a bath. I told her that we did it all the time.

22

The Boy Who Carried Bricks

She asked me if my mom had been working all day and is that why she was asleep. I told her no, Mom was sick and had taken some pills so she would feel better, and they had made her sleepy. The lady kept writing even after I had stopped talking. She wrote for a long time, but eventually she put her pen back in her purse and put her notebook on the stack of folders on the table. She then told us that she was going to sit with us until Mom came out of the emergency room.

When Mom finally returned, she was carrying Dejohn; my brother was wrapped in bandages, like a little mummy. Still crying Mom signed some papers and loaded us in the car and took us home. I thought the worse was over. I couldn't have been more wrong.

Once we got home, Mom laid Dejohn down on the couch and started screaming at Lavell and me about telling the DHS worker what had happened. She said thanks to our big mouths the courts were going to take all of us away from her.

"You are never to tell DHS anything," she hissed.

Our telling DHS the truth that night was the beginning of many investigations into our home life. The DHS caseworkers would come to wherever we were living and do random home visits. Many times they found us home alone playing in a dirty, roach-infested house with no food. Time and time again, they took reports and left us the same way they found us. I knew my mom was scared of them, but I truly didn't understand why. Nothing ever seemed to come from what they found or saw. No matter how bad.

To keep them off her back, Mom started dropping us off at my grandparents' house when she went out at night. My grandparents lived in Stillwater but for some reason were not on speaking terms with my mom at the time. They agreed to keep us nonetheless.

But for Mom, nights too often turned into days. She would take us to our grandparents telling them and us that she would be back in the morning. Time after time, however, she did not show up till days later. When she did finally return, she and my grandpa would argue as Grandpa tried to explain to her that she was not being fair to her parents or her children.

Mom always tried to turn it back on Grandpa, saying he just did not care about her or her children.

Still by 1978, we were practically living with our grandparents and rarely saw Mom.

I was eight years old.

Chapter 7
Meet the Carters

I am not sure how or why but my two cousins, Martina and Mario, ended up living with my grandparents about this time, too. I could not tell you where their mother, my Aunt Faye, lived as she rarely came to town to see them.

What I do remember about Aunt Faye is that she claimed to be very religious. When she visited, she would always read her Bible and talk a lot about God as if we were heathens that needed saving. She may have been correct about us needing to be saved, but I didn't understand why she was so hard on us when she did not appear to be able to keep her own house in order. I also never figured out why she did not let Martina and Mario live with her.

At this point, Martina was the oldest of the grandchildren living with my grandparents. Pretty and popular, she was always in the middle of some drama with either one of her much older inappropriate boyfriends or one of her many girlfriends.

Mario was about three years younger than Martina and had a different father. He was quiet, tough, handsome, and as cool as they come. Mario and I were a month and a half apart in age and had nothing in common—I was awkward, split-toothed, and shy, but he allowed me to hang out with him from time to time.

This was a welcome break for me, because my oldest brother, Lavell, had taken up with some bad kids and begun to change for the worse. My early memories of Lavell are of him trying to take care of us when Mom was gone or passed out, despite being just a child himself. I remember once he figured out how to open a can of spinach so we wouldn't go hungry that night. He dressed us, bathed the little ones, and watched over us. I remember thinking of him as our protector.

But by the time he turned nine or ten that had all changed. He began to use every opportunity to remind us that he was the oldest. He started picking on us and humiliating us in front of his friends by calling us names and hitting us until we cried. Lavell was smart enough to never be disrespectful to adults, but he never applied himself at school. Instead, he used his smarts to figure out how to break into vending machines for pop and candy.

With Mom rarely home, he started sneaking out and staying out all night with his friends—breaking into gas stations and bicycle shops and vandalizing buildings. I hadn't thought life could get any worse for us but I was wrong. Losing the Lavell I knew and loved as a child was a blow that still hurts.

Almost two years younger than Lavell, I was next in line, an athletic, average-sized kid but so prone to crying that everyone called me a crybaby. I was self-conscious about being poor, and I had big gaps between my front, top and bottom teeth that kept me from smiling. I might not have been a sullen child but I am sure I looked like one.

In grade school, I had few friends and spent a lot of time by myself. I wasn't book smart and did terrible in most subjects, especially math and reading. Aware that I did not read well, I hated reading aloud. And so before my turn to read in front of the class came up, I always made sure I did something to get myself sent out into the hall. On my best days, I disrupted class by constantly getting up out of my seat and talking back to the teacher and picking fights during recess and calling kids names. Needless to say, I spent a lot of time in the principal and counselor's offices. Ironically, I craved attention and wanted people to like me but had no idea how to get either. What I wouldn't have given for a teacher who recognized my actions for what they were: a cry for help.

One thing Lavell and I had going for us was good health; our siblings were not so lucky. The twins, Watell and Kesha, both had severe asthma and, like me, were missing their front teeth. Both were also allergic to dust, cigarette smoke, mold, and grass. This kept Watell, a wispy athletic boy and one of the fastest kids in the school, from participating in sports, but it never stopped any of our relatives from smoking around him or his sister at home. Both twins were hospitalized more than once for severe asthma attacks, and one time my mom actually found Watell on the bed unconscious—he spent several weeks in the hospital recovering from that episode.

Watell had few friends but was well liked by everyone. The same could not be said for his twin. Kesha was loud and was always looking to start a fight. A tomboy who never bothered to fix her hair, she wore boy clothes and cussed like a sailor (something she learned from the older women in our family). The friends she had were friends because they were either scared of her or just like her. Still, she adored her twin and would fight anyone who dared look at Watell wrong.

The youngest of the Carter siblings was Dejohn. He was, by far, the smartest of us all. He had a gap in his top teeth but not in the bottom. He loved tinkering with things and was always taking something apart and putting it back together. I remember once when he was older he figured out how to rig a television set to a dresser drawer: if you opened the drawer the TV came on, and you could control the volume by how far you pulled out the drawer.

Although none of us wore clean clothes, Dejohn always seemed to have on the dirtiest clothes he could find. His socks never matched, and he could have cared less. He did well in school and had lots of friends, but sadly he would grow up to follow in Lavell's footsteps.

At the head of the Carter family was my mom. Tall and fit with soft hair, she was the prettiest woman I knew. But being the mother of five children from four different men says a lot about what she thought of herself. Looking back, I realize now she was desperate to find someone worthy of her, and yet she was patently unable to see the men she dated for what they were. She wanted a strong, stable man in her life and yet she settled for men who were unemployed with criminal records. Many times she assured us that the men she brought home were good men that she loved—knights in shining armor, men eager to be a father to us—because that is what she so wanted to believe.

In reality, the men were anything but good and she did not love them, and I knew it, even if she could not see it. I never understood how she could move strange, unemployed men, sometimes even felons, into her house to take food out of the mouths of her own five hungry children.

Oh, the men would tell great tales of how they were going to help her pay bills and be fathers to us. But I learned early on that their stories were nothing more than lies. Blinded by dreams of being married to a good man, my mother failed to see them for what they really were.

Still, no matter what she put us through, I loved my mom more than anything and I always wanted the best for her. I wanted to believe she wanted the same for us. And I dreamed someday she would wise up and look with her heart at the men she exposed us to.

Chapter 8
The Good Teacher

By 1979, we were living with my mom a few blocks from our grandparents' house on the east side of Stillwater and attending Highland Park Elementary. I was in Mrs. Smith's fourth-grade class, and on this particular day, like most days, I was talking during reading time to her chagrin.

"Stop talking Alton," Mrs. Smith said. Her normally tense face tightening even more.

I ignored her.

"Alton, I said, stop talking."

A tall, thin lady with brown hair, Mrs. Smith was a very structured teacher who, fundamentally, was a solid educator but one with little patience for unruly students. She was easily frustrated and did not hesitate to send her students into the hallway. I practically lived there while I was in her class.

After several more stern warnings to stop talking, Mrs. Smith walked up to my desk, slammed her hand on the desk, and yet again told me to leave her class as she had so many times before. But today something was different, and I could sense it. I knew I had pushed her past her breaking point when she grabbed me by the arm and started dragging me towards the hallway.

I resisted just enough to make her even more upset. She squeezed my arm harder, and the dragging turned into pushing. She stopped at the door and opened it with her other hand; before I exited I took one look back at the class only to see all the students staring at me. I could tell that they too had had enough of me. I was embarrassed and so ashamed at being literally dragged out of class. It did not escape me that my fellow classmates looked at me as though they were glad that I was leaving.

Once we were in the hallway, Mrs. Smith pushed me down on the floor and starting yelling that she had had enough of my behavior and was tired of being unable to teach her class because I was such a troublemaker.

"I have tried everything I could to help you Alton," she said, "but you don't appreciate any of it."

I didn't contradict her. And the more she yelled, the madder she got. I don't know if she was trying to elicit a response from me or not, but she was yelling so loud that other teachers were now opening their doors to see what was going on. Right then, a door across the hall opened and out came Mrs. Thompson.

Mrs. Thompson was another fourth-grade teacher whom I had seen many times around school. I remembered her because during recess she was always nice to everyone. She was average build, tall, with curly blonde hair and a peaceful demeanor. A lot of the teachers at school yelled and screamed at students but not Mrs. Thompson. She made a point of walking around and interacting with kids—even those not in her own class. That day she came to see what was going on between me and Mrs. Smith, I was never happier to see anyone in my life.

Although I deserved the scolding I was getting, I also wanted someone to stop it, and I was hoping it would be her. Mrs. Thompson walked across the hall and asked Mrs. Smith what the problem was, and without hesitation, Mrs. Smith answered: "I can't stand Alton anymore—I want him out of my class!"

Mrs. Thompson looked down at me, took me by the hand, and said, "I'll take him."

At first I was confused about what had just happened. It wasn't until Mrs. Thompson went into my classroom and came out with my belongings, that I realized I was no longer in Mrs. Smith's class. Mrs. Thompson walked me over to her room and introduced me to her students then she directed me to a desk right next to hers.

In Mrs. Smith's class, I had sat at the back of the class, and now I was at the front, right next to the teacher. It may sound funny, but I felt privileged to sit next to the teacher that all the students liked.

Mrs. Thompson quietly told me she realized I was having a bad day and so she wanted me to just sit and observe until the bell rang.

"We'll start fresh tomorrow," she said.

It was as if someone had thrown me in the trash, and Mrs. Thompson dug me out and dusted me off. You would have thought I would be grateful. And I was. But I also didn't trust what had just happened. I told myself Mrs. Thompson had made a mistake and that she wouldn't want me in her class anymore than Mrs. Smith had, and then I set out to prove it. Our honeymoon lasted all of two days. By the third, I was back to throwing pencils and talking out of turn and overall testing her patience.

Because of my behavior, I missed a lot of recess, but Mrs. Thompson never yelled at me, never banished me to the hallway, never sent me to the principal's office like Mrs. Smith had. In fact, when I had to miss recess, Mrs. Thompson usually stayed in the classroom with me, trying to get me to open up about what was bothering me.

Mrs. Thompson knew there were problems at home, and she kept asking me why I was misbehaving in class. I had a truckload of reasons and excuses for why I acted the way I did, but I didn't dare tell her any of them. My home life was bad enough; I did not need my mom whipping me because I had told someone the truth about it. I still remembered the lesson of the DHS lady and Dejohn.

So, every time Mrs. Thompson asked me what was wrong, I stared at the ground and just shook my head. Day after day, I pretty much tested every ounce of patience Mrs. Thompson had. Having convinced myself that I wasn't worth saving, I could not understand why this teacher would try to help me. If my own mother did not care about me nor my brothers and sister, why would Mrs. Thompson care about a poor, black boy who did nothing but give her grief?

Yet in reality, I wanted badly to tell her what was going on at home: That our mom left us hungry and alone all the time, that I had seen strange men beat my mom more times than I could count, that my mom took prescription drugs that left her passed out in the middle of the day, leaving my siblings and me to fend for ourselves.

I wanted to show her my scars from the beatings I had gotten. I wanted to describe to her in detail the times I would come home and find my mother on her hands and knees picking things up off the floor and trying to smoke them because she thought they were crack. I wanted to tell Mrs. Thompson everything. But I just couldn't.

It wasn't that I was scared. I just cared more about my mom than she cared about me, and I knew if I told on my mom they would take us away from her. At a time in my life when my mother should have been protecting me, every day I protected her by lying to anyone who dared ask what was wrong with me. As much as I wanted to tell Mrs. Thompson everything, I told myself she did not really care or want to know how bad things were at home for me and my brothers and sister.

What could she do even if I told her, I thought. *DHS has been to our house a thousand times and never cared enough to save us. And that is their job!*

Truth be told, I was afraid of getting too close to anyone, much less a teacher who really didn't know me. So I gave Mrs. Thompson every reason in the world to kick me out of her class, and to say that I was surprised that she never did would be an understatement.

Still I was missing a lot of recess. One particular afternoon while my classmates played outside, Mrs. Thompson yet again stayed in with me, trying to get me to talk. My only response to her obvious concern for me was to stare at the floor.

"Do you know why you're not outside playing with the others?" she asked.

The Boy Who Carried Bricks

"Yeah, because you don't like me because I'm black," I said.

And this time I raised my head and looked her in the eye to see her reaction. I saw my teacher blink to stop the tears, but it did not stop them from falling. She abruptly stood and, without saying another word, ran from the classroom.

I just sat there. I knew what I had said was wrong, horribly unfair even, but I told myself, *maybe now she will leave me alone.* For the rest of the day, I sat at my desk and never lifted my pencil or my head.

When the bell rang for school to be out, I ran out of class and down the block to my grandparents' house. Dejohn was outside, and as we played catch, I thought about what I had said to Mrs. Thompson. I knew it was wrong, but my family said that sort of thing all the time. Anytime anyone in my family got in trouble with the police, their go-to excuse was, "You're picking on me because I'm black." I had always thought that was lame, especially because most of the times my relative had done the deed and were really just mad about having been caught.

Now I had gone and leveled the same lame accusation against one of the nicest teachers I had ever known. I felt sick about what I had done. But I sure wasn't going to tell Mrs. Thompson I was sorry. *Who knows where that might lead?* I told myself.

I had just finished working my way to that conclusion, when a car pulled up in the driveway. Dejohn and I paused playing catch long enough to see who it was. The driver's door swung open, and Mrs. Thompson stepped out. She called me over, saying she wanted to talk to me. I wasn't sure what was going on, but I was not about to let a teacher intimidate me, especially in front of my little brother. So I strutted over to her with my arms swaying away from my body, like a gunslinger's, shoulders pulled back, and chin up in the air—defiant to the end. When I was a few feet away from her, Mrs. Thompson told me she had someone she wanted me to meet.

"I don't think you've ever met my husband," she said.

Before I could confirm or deny it, the passenger car door swung open, and her husband climbed out and stuck out his hand.

"Hello Alton," he said kindly, with a small smile.

I was in complete shock. I could no more shake his hand than I could talk. I stood there for what seemed like forever, staring, with my mouth open, at Mrs. Thompson and her African-American husband.

Once again, I wanted with every fiber of my being to tell Mrs. Thompson I was sorry, but I just couldn't. Instead, I took off running, hiding behind the house until she and her husband were gone.

That night, I went to sleep on the floor a different person. True, most of the world, including my own mom and family, might not care if I was dead or alive. But I now knew without a doubt that one person did.

Nonetheless, I went to school the next day expecting my teacher to give me away just as Mrs. Smith did when I embarrassed her. I would not have blamed Mrs. Thompson if she had.

Instead, when I stepped into her classroom, she pulled me aside.

"Do you know why you missed recess yesterday, Alton?" she asked.

"Yes, Mrs. Thompson," I said. "I missed recess because I misbehaved in class."

She smiled. And so did I. And then Mrs. Thompson went on to tell me that she knew my home life was terrible and that it was important for me to know it was not my fault.

"But Alton, it also is not my fault nor the fault of any of your classmates," she said. "You need to learn to take responsibility for your own actions and quit making excuses. Your problems at school have nothing to do with the color of your skin."

Then Mrs. Thompson bent down and looked me straight in the face and wrapped her arms around me and held me for what seemed like forever.

For the first time in my life, I felt like I was worth something.

Chapter 9
Throwing Apples

Mom always spent more time trying to find men than she did taking care of us. Neighbors and schoolteachers, like Mrs. Thompson, did what they could to help, but it is difficult for someone to fix what they do not know about.

And what our teachers did not know was that more often than not, our little house was without electricity or gas, which left us without heat in the winter and air-conditioning in the stifling hot Oklahoma summer. In the wintertime, my siblings and I would bundle up in clothes and huddle together on the floor where we slept, sharing blankets to keep warm. Summers were no more forgiving, and when the temperatures hit triple digits, there was little we could do to escape the heat. Mom was always late paying the bills.

Growing up unsupervised and perpetually hungry led us to do crazy things, if only because getting into trouble was sometimes the only form of distraction available from our miserable life at home.

At those times, we were like a gang of little kids, creating chaos and leaving a trail of destruction wherever we went. Every so often, Lavell would actually let Dejohn and me run the streets with his friends. One particular night, one of Lavell's friends came up with the brilliant idea to throw apples at cars as they passed by to see how many we could hit.

First we needed apples, so we walked across town to a park that had an apple tree. (I know what you're thinking: Why couldn't boys willing to walk miles to cause trouble not exert the same energy to do something constructive or even silly but not destructive? My answer: We had no role models for that. No one had ever taught us how to funnel our youthful energy into anything positive. And we never had the books or stories to read that might have shown us another way.)

That night we each picked three or four apples at a time, walked to the middle of the street, formed a line, and waited for a car to approach. When a car drew near, we would all throw our apples as high as we could, straight up in the air, and make a mad dash for the park. We hid behind trees and watched the apples rain down on the unsuspecting cars. Most of the time we missed, but a few times the apples found their mark.

The secret to hitting the target wasn't necessarily more apples. The most productive attack we ever had, found each of us with only two apples to throw. The car was about half a block away when we let the apples fly straight to the moon. Then like normal, we ran and hid behind trees near the road. Only unlike all the times before, it seemed that every apple scored a hit as the car passed by.

Boom! Boom! We heard the apples hit the hood of the car.

And then we heard a crash! One of the apples had hit the windshield and shattered it. The driver slammed on his brakes and jumped out of the car screaming and cussing at us. We just laughed at him until he reached back inside and pulled out a shotgun and fired off two shots.

None of us could say for sure if he had aimed at us, because we were running as fast as we could down the street. You do a lot of running away from people when your playground is the streets, even on the basically quiet streets of a relatively idyllic university town like Stillwater. You also develop a different relationship with the local police. My brothers and I had seen so many police officers knocking on our front door looking for one of our uncles or dragging one of our inebriated uncles home that we didn't really take them all that seriously. About this time, we began having our own encounters with the police, only we rarely got caught because when the police cars showed up, we all just scattered. If by some chance a policeman managed to catch one of us, the worst outcome was usually a lecture and a ride home in the back of his police car.

Before long, the police knew us all by name and where each of us lived—to this day you can say the name Carter to a Stillwater policeman and chances are, they will know who you mean. It was a dubious honor to say the least.

Anyone who has lived the life can tell you that the childish antics on the street start small and harmless and escalate to stealing and vandalism . . . or worse. My brother Lavell and his friends were already pretty far down that slippery slope headed to nowhere good, and I might well have followed them had one night not changed me forever. It was about one in the morning, and we were prowling the Oklahoma State University campus a good two miles from where we lived. Lavell had grown tired of walking and suggested we find a bicycle to ride home instead.

"Look at all these bikes," he said. "I bet we can find one or two unlocked."

Sure enough, he was right. Within minutes we each had a bike and were headed east for home. Eight boys riding single file down a sidewalk in the middle of the night is not a normal sight, even on a college campus. I don't know if someone called 9-1-1 or what, but suddenly a police car came out of nowhere flashing its lights. We scattered as usual, pedaling as fast as we could on the stolen bikes, when I heard the police officer yell, "Freeze!"

And for some reason I stopped.

Still in his car, the officer pulled up alongside me and got out with his gun drawn. He pointed his gun at me and told me to get down on the ground. I was so scared I could not move. But I realize now he did not know that. He grabbed me by the scruff of my neck and threw me down on the hood of his patrol car. What happened next caused me to never run the streets with my brother and friends again: The officer put the barrel of the gun to my temple and told me to give him a reason to blow my head off.

While part of me knew he would not, could not shoot me—*This was America, right? We have laws against such things! Little boys don't get shot for joyriding on a bike!*—the rest of me was so scared that I started to bawl.

"Stop crying," the police officer said. "If you want to be a big bad criminal you had better get used to having a gun pointed at you."

I never ran the streets again.

Chapter 10
Living Hungry

Through the years, more than one of our teachers on different occasions made the trip to our house late at night to bring us groceries. Our rumbling stomachs were the background music for their classrooms; it must have been quite clear to them that we rarely had breakfast. The days we did, breakfast was cold cereal and water because the perennial lack of electricity kept the milk in the refrigerator spoiled.

Showing up hungry and late to school was part of the Carter family routine. One semester, after being late to school several times and arriving hungry, the cafeteria lady told us from now on to come see her no matter what time we showed up at school, and she would fix us something to eat. Thanks to Uncle Sam, we also received a free lunch at school; often that would be our last meal of the day, especially at the end of the month.

At the beginning of month, Mom would buy what little groceries she could afford. By the middle of the month, the refrigerator would be empty, and the cupboards would hold only a few canned goods and a little moldy bread. Come the last of week of the month even that was gone. Hunger and being left at home unsupervised were the two key reasons why DHS eventually took us away from Mom and sent us to live with my grandparents.

I will never forget the last time the caseworker came to do a home visit. By this time, DHS had come to our house so many times I had lost count, but the home visits had never resulted in any improvement that I could see. This afternoon when the DHS caseworker showed up, our front door was wide open, so she just came right on in. She found me in the kitchen using a butcher's knife to pry open a can of food—it had been a long time since Lavell was nice enough to open a can when his little brothers and sister were hungry. The DHS worker asked if she could speak with our mom.

"She's not home," I said.

In fact, we had not seen our mother for a few days, but we knew better than to tell the DHS lady that. We had not forgotten the lesson learned in that hospital waiting room.

The caseworker looked around the house a bit and then left. The next day we got ourselves up and went to school late and dirty and hungry as usual. We were walking home from school that afternoon when the same DHS worker pulled up beside us and asked us to get in the car. We did as we were told, uncertain as to where she was taking us. After a few minutes, we arrived at a white house located on the corner of Eighth and West streets. It was the Payne County Youth Shelter. We followed her inside where she sat us down and explained that we were going to spend the night there and that we would not be going home for a few days. She introduced us to the shelter parents and then left them to show us our beds for the night.

In a strange way, I was excited about this new development because I could not remember the last time I had slept in a bed, let alone a bed by myself. I asked if I had heard right.

"You mean I get to sleep in this bed all by myself?" I asked.

"Yes, Alton. This is your bed while you are staying at the shelter," the shelter mom said.

I spent the whole evening in bed just thinking how wonderful it was that I was going to finally get to sleep off the ground, on a soft mattress, all by myself, under warm covers in a warm house. The only time I left my bed was to eat dinner. After that the shelter parents told us it was time to hit the sack because we had a big day tomorrow. That is when it hit me. As excited as I was about having a bed, I wanted to go home. *I wonder if Mom knows we're gone*, I thought.

The idea that our mom might be wondering where we were upset me, and I went to the shelter parents and asked if I could go home.

"Not tonight, Alton. You have to stay here for the night."

"I need to go home in case my mom comes home," I told them.

When the answer was still no, I tried to dart past them, out the door. When they caught me, I started kicking and screaming that I wanted to go home.

The more they told me I could not go home, the more upset I became. I began running around the room trying to find a way out of the house. I became so upset I had to be restrained. The shelter mom held me tight for what seemed like forever until I finally calmed down. That night I cried myself to sleep in the big, now lonely bed that just hours before I had never wanted to leave.

Morning brought a big breakfast and clean clothes and a trip to the courthouse. The DHS caseworker escorted us into an office connected to the courtroom. It seemed as if we were there for hours, before a woman came in and said the judge was ready for us. We were seated at a long table to the right of the judge, when our mom arrived. We had not known she would be there; we had not seen her for days. She and another woman were seated behind a long table to the left of the judge. The judge began to question my mom and his questions seemed to bother her. I did not understand what was happening but the longer it went on the more upset she became.

Finally the questions ended. And the judge announced his decision. "It is the court's decision to remove all five children from the home as you are not fit to take care of them."

Mom began crying so loud the judge had the bailiff drag her out of the courtroom. In the later part of 1979, we were removed from the care of my mom and placed into our maternal grandparents' custody.

Chapter 11
Grandparents

My grandparents were the foundation of our entire family, and they spent all of their lives taking care of their children and grandchildren. Most of my cousins spent more time with Grandma and Grandpa than they ever did with their own parents.

For most of my grandma's life, she cleaned houses and ironed clothes for people. She was about five feet tall with unruly gray hair. She had no teeth and always wore muumuu dresses that skimmed her knees when she stood. The only time she ever dressed up was for one of Grandpa's work events. For such times, she had a wig—it was far easier than having one's hair done, according to Grandma. Her only vanity was her false teeth—she never wanted to be seen in public without them.

She was profane (I would contend that Grandma taught us all how to cuss), and spent most Friday nights in her broken, brown recliner, drinking beer and listening to the blues. Most days she would start drinking midafternoon, and by nightfall be so drunk she would slump over in her chair. I never knew how she kept from falling out of it.

The Boy Who Carried Bricks

Generally, Grandma was sweet and loving, but she had a temper. Lenient on most things, she had only one rule that she insisted on: always be home before dark. Lavell got around it by being home before dark then sneaking out the second floor where the grandchildren slept after Grandma went to bed.

We knew Grandma loved us, but truth be told, she was always more partial to her sons, while her daughters were closer to Grandpa. Grandma always defended her sons—no matter how bad things were or how badly they messed up. Her unconditional support for them established a dependent relationship that saw her grown sons rarely move out. If they did manage to leave home, it was never long before they were back. My uncles were always given the beds while the grandchildren slept on the hard floor. Grandma would have given her last penny to be able to save each and every one of her sons from experiencing any hardship in life.

My grandpa, on the other hand, was a hard-working, soft-spoken man. Bald and standing about six foot tall, he was a well-respected worker at Central Mailing at OSU, and he also refereed local football, baseball, and basketball games year-round. His day job required him to dress in slacks and dress shirts; his referee work required a uniform, but around the house Grandpa could be found wearing coveralls.

He drank a beer from time to time, but I never saw Grandpa drunk, nor did he ever use bad language. Although we rarely attended church, he was one of the greatest Christians I have ever known. He did not talk about God much, but he lived his faith by example. He was wise and always encouraged us to do the right thing. Unlike the rest of my family, he never blamed anyone for his problems.

Unfortunately, Grandpa was also gone a lot, and I believe he stayed away from home because he did not want to deal with the drama. It was easy to see he was disappointed about how his children had turned out. While he had worked hard for everything he had, he watched his children do all they could to get something for nothing.

My grandparents did not fight a lot, but when they did, it was usually about something my uncles, aunt, or mother had or had not done. Grandpa never said a word about the way Grandma drank beer or cussed or disciplined us, but we could tell he did not agree with it.

Riding in the car with him, away from the chaos of home and Grandma, he would tell me stories from his childhood, stories about being the only black guy on a baseball team and having to eat out back when the players stopped at restaurants on the road. He told me many similar stories about growing up black in Oklahoma, all different yet oddly alike, though somehow he never sounded bitter about the past. And that was telling to me.

The rest of our family was bitter to the core. My aunts, uncles, siblings, mother, and grandmother disliked almost all white people, and used racial slurs like some folks use adjectives. They called each other "n-----," which I never understood. If they had exhibited even the slightest sign of self-respect, I might have thought they were being political when they yelled the racial epithet at each other, trying as they say to take the power out of a hateful word. But they did not have a political bone in their bodies.

Grandpa hated profanity and racial slurs. He always told me people who cussed were ignorant and lazy and not smart enough to use a better word to describe how they felt. He also said there was never a reason to name call. Grandpa saw the good in everybody and was always willing to help anyone who crossed his path—no matter their color or station. One of the most important lessons Grandpa ever taught me has always stayed with me: "Hang out with people who are better than you, Alton," he told me more than once. "Play sports with athletes who are better than you, sit by classmates who are smarter than you, hang out with kids who make better choices than you."

When I asked him why, Grandpa said doing so would encourage me to be better . . . to be the best version of me.

"It will lift you up, Alton. It will keep you from being dragged down by people who are making bad choices."

I did not understand it then, but later I figured out that Grandpa was telling me not to hang out with my family, or people like them.

Grandpa also taught me how to find joy in the little pleasures of life. I never heard Grandpa lament not being richer or having nicer things. I think in his own eyes he was Oklahoma rich because he had two trucks, even if the ole green Chevy almost always had to be jump-started. The second truck was a tan pickup with a camper in its bed. It wasn't in very good condition either, but Grandpa used it for his trips to away games.

The times I went with him to referee, I never actually went into the stadiums or ballparks. He always just parked where he could see the camper and I would watch the game from atop the cab. We couldn't afford to eat out on our road trips, so he always packed sandwiches, ginger snap cookies, and Shasta. Those trips with Grandpa were the closest I came to normalcy as a boy.

At home, he spent most of his time outside tinkering, mainly because he could not abide confrontation. Anytime anyone in the house started arguing or fighting, Grandpa would get up, put on his coveralls, and go outside. He was outside a lot.

His approach to discipline differed from Grandma's as well. Grandpa never laid a hand on any of us and never cursed at us, but he was always quick to threaten a spanking.

On the surface, my grandpa seemed happy and content with his life, but deep down I know he had to be anything but. He worked day and night while his three adult sons could not hold a job and his two adult daughters could not take care of their own children. The police had to be called to the house that he had so proudly built, at least twice a week for one reason or another. The man had to be hungry for a little peace and quiet; I think that is what the ballpark gave him. I can't help thinking that anyone else would have walked away from it all, from all of us. But for some reason Grandpa stayed. Maybe he believed someday things would be different for all of us. He was what you call a perennial optimist.

I know he believed in me. He took time with me because I showed an interest in him and what he tried to teach me about people and life. He also claimed to have named me, supposedly after the man who gave him his first job after moving from Denver, Colorado, to Stillwater. I never knew if that was true or not, but I told myself I must have been special to my grandpa from the very start if he had given me my name.

There was only one thing Grandpa could do that bothered me, and that was when he went anywhere at night without me. When the uncles and cousins and Grandma were fighting and arguing, he would sometimes walk out the front door to show he didn't approve of what was going on. Other times he would quietly leave out the back door, and no one would know he was gone. It didn't matter his reason for leaving, I did not want to be there without him; I wanted to go with him. Being with him away from the house was safe, safe from the violence and the alcohol and the chaos that was my life.

Chapter 12
The Wishing Game

We may not have gotten along. We may have put each other in danger. But growing up so poor in so many ways had the odd result of making the bond between my two cousins and my brothers, sister, and me incredibly strong. We shared almost everything because there was not enough of anything to go around. Our clothes rarely fit, most had holes in them, and more often than not they came from the Salvation Army.

Our wardrobe matched the house we lived in. Grandpa had remodeled it through the years using discarded wood and fixtures. Grandpa would see a house being demolished, and he would call the owner and ask if he could sift through the refuse piles for salvageable lumber before it was hauled away to the dump. Whatever Grandpa found he hauled home to our backyard. With at least one broken down car at any given time, the rusting washing machine, the empty beer cans, and the old mowers scattered about the chest-high grass, a few stacks of two-by-fours was hardly a cause for concern. Grandpa paid me a nickel a board to pull nails out of the used lumber so he could reuse it on his various unorthodox remodeling projects.

As we grew older, one of the most uncomfortable things about living with Grandma and Grandpa was that their house sat only a block from Highland Park Elementary. Most kids had to walk by it to get to school. We knew it was a neighborhood eyesore and the butt of our classmates' jokes, so our daily mutual goal was to leave for school late or extremely early so no one would see us come out of it.

Misery, as they say, loves company, and shared objectives like getting to school without being teased about where we lived helped tighten the bonds of childhood. And inside our grandparents' ram-shackle house, the seven of us actually managed to make a few good childhood memories, too.

We played "Cowboys and Indians" and "Cops and Robbers" outside under the stars and inside, our favorite game was "The Wishing Game." We played it late at night long after the adults had gone to bed and only when our Uncle Stevie was not home. We would gather and wrap ourselves in our blankets, the same ones that most nights served as our beds, and form a small tight circle on the floor. Being the oldest cousin, Martina always went first.

The game is best described by this poem I wrote many years later:

The Wishing Game

I remember when I was young,
In a circle we would play a game.
Taking turns we make a wish.
No wish would be the same.
Our wishes were unlimited.
A wish for something to eat,
A wish for a new bike,
New shoes for our feet,
A wish for a new house,
A new car would be nice,
A wish to rid us of roaches,

The Boy Who Carried Bricks

And a wish to take the mice.
Wishing never solved our problems,
Or made them go away.
We never got what we wished for,
And still we wished each day.

My very favorite wish was to wish that I had a million dollars so I could buy my mom a house and we could live with her. It is true we rarely saw even our smallest wishes come true, but that simple game gave us hope that someday we would have what most kids took for granted.

Chapter 13
The Uncles

Three uncles lived with us at my grandparents' house: Billy, David, and Stevie. Uncle Billy was the youngest, and moved in with Grandma and Grandpa after he got out of prison and had no place to live. He was about six feet tall, weighed 230 pounds, and had an even heavier chip on his shoulder. Uncle Billy only came out of his room to use the bathroom or get something to eat; he only left the house when he had to check in with his probation officer.

Basically, Uncle Billy had exchanged one prison for another of his own making. He kept his room clean and organized, like he kept himself. His hair was always fixed, and he never wore anything that hadn't been ironed. He didn't drink much alcohol, but he smoked a lot of pot—there was no mistaking the smell coming from his bedroom.

Uncle Billy was married, and his wife lived at my grandparents' on and off. She would move in, stay until she grew tired of his beatings, and then move out, only so she could forgive him and start the cycle of drama again. We lived under the same roof but none of us little kids ever got to know Uncle Billy. Proof you can, indeed, be a stranger in your own home. Uncle David was the oldest of the uncles and a harmless drunk. He could always be found doing one of three things: drinking booze, reading a newspaper, or sharing his various conspiracy theories. Short, wiry, intelligent, and paranoid, he spent most mornings watching the news and reading the paper before his drinking day commenced.

Unlike Uncle Billy, Uncle David cared little about what he looked like. His clothes never matched, his shoes had holes, and his hair was never fixed. He only left the house to buy more alcohol. And by the time he returned from the liquor store, he was always drunk. Yet I liked Uncle David. He was never violent, he was nice to his nieces and nephews, and I thought his conspiracy theories were funny (my favorite had to do with the government putting computer chips in our heads as part of a mind-control experiment).

Unable to watch much TV because the adults always controlled the channel, my cousins, siblings, and I spent hours watching the slapstick comedy that was Drunk Uncle David. Our uncle would walk through the house, like he was on a ship rolling in heavy waves; the rocking motion caused him to constantly knock things over and he fell down the stairs more times than he walked down them. It was like having our own Laurel and Hardy.

More than once, Uncle David passed out drunk with a cigarette in his mouth, and we gathered round to watch as the cigarette burned down to his lips. When it reached them, he would jump up screaming, and we would laugh until we couldn't breathe.

Both Uncle Billy and Uncle David were classic cautionary tales for a young boy, but they were also relatively harmless. The same could not be said for our Uncle Stevie. Rarely to be seen in the daytime, Uncle Stevie was about six foot tall and 180 pounds. Intelligent and vain, he sported a handlebar mustache that curled up to his nostrils. There were two Uncle Stevies: one was fun; the other was downright mean, as I was to learn the hard way.

Chapter 14
Breakfast of Champions

It is said that children of alcoholics learn to read people like a farmer can read the wind and know a storm is brewing. In both cases, it is a matter of survival. But bad storms only come along every so often. Living with an alcoholic parent or relative is like being on storm patrol 24/7. It frays the nerves. It is exhausting. And it means any day can turn deadly in an instant.

One morning I was in the kitchen eating a bowl of cereal when Uncle Stevie came in to make himself some breakfast. Without a word to me, he went about scrambling some eggs on the stove before taking a seat at the table across from me and starting to eat.

"You want some?" he asked, looking up from his plate.

Before I could answer, he scraped some of his eggs onto another plate and slid them across the table, landing it right in front of me.

"Eggs are muscle food," he said. "They'll make even a sissy like you strong."

I knew better than to reply, so I concentrated on eating my cereal and the eggs he had given me. They tasted good, even served with my uncle's steady stream of insults about my manhood or lack thereof.

Looking back now, I blame the eggs. Any other time I like to think I would have seen it coming. But the eggs were good. I was, as always, hungry. And I was lulled into a false sense of security. So I didn't think anything of it when Uncle Stevie got up, went to the stove, and turned the burner back on. He stood there for a few minutes as the flame heated up the grate. I finished eating my cereal and eggs.

When I went to place my dirty dishes in the sink, I brushed by Uncle Stevie, still standing at the stove. He grabbed me just below my elbow. I stopped.

"If you were a real man you could hold your arm over this burner without flinching," he said.

To prove it, he stuck his arm a few inches above the burner grate and held it there for a few seconds before pulling it away.

"Come on, Alton," said Uncle Stevie. "You don't want to be a sissy anymore do you?"

I knew it wasn't really a question. And as much as I didn't want to prove myself, I knew I didn't have an option; Uncle Stevie was going to make me do what he wanted no matter what I said.

Better just get it over with, I thought, cursing myself for having stayed in the kitchen after he showed up when I should have known better.

Hesitantly and slowly, I stuck my arm out over the hot burner. As I flinched from the first blast of heat, Uncle Stevie grabbed my forearm and shoved it down onto the burner grate. I screamed in agony, jerking my arm away from my uncle. As I did, some of my skin was left behind on the grate, and that skin continued to burn, giving off the horrible stench usually reserved for crematoriums.

I ran to the sink to put some water on my burn, but the pain knocked me to the kitchen floor and I began sobbing. A few feet away from me, Uncle Stevie stood, shaking his head with a look of disappointment on his face.

"You're *always* going to be a sissy," he said.

And with that, he turned and walked out of the kitchen. Meanwhile, my screams had drawn Grandma who wanted to know what had happened to make me cry out. Before I could answer her, Uncle

Stevie came back in and told her I had burned my arm while cooking eggs. I didn't dare say otherwise.

As Grandma proceeded to doctor my burn with the flesh from one of her Aloe Vera plants, I sat mum. Uncle Stevie never strayed from the kitchen until we were through to make sure I didn't try to tell Grandma what had happened.

Sadly, as much as I wanted to tell her what Uncle Stevie had done, I knew she would never believe me even if I told her; like I said before, in Grandma's world her sons trumped grandchildren: they could do no wrong.

So I kept my mouth shut until she had finished treating my burn. And when she was finished, I went downstairs to find my grandpa, but he was nowhere to be found, so I spent the rest of the day outside, far away from Uncle Stevie.

Chapter 15
Blueberry Pie & Mowers

I normally did whatever I could to stay away from Uncle Stevie—we all did—but not having any friends of my own, I was forced to spend a lot of time at my grandparents' house. On the rare occasion that Lavell allowed me to hang out with him and his friends in public, the privilege came at a high price, but it was better than being alone. Or so I told myself.

Lavell and his friends teased me relentlessly, and forced me to do stupid things—to refuse was to be sent home. Most of their pranks were silly, but on more than one occasion they made me do things that were illegal. And sometimes I didn't even see it coming.

"Hey Alton, I have to go home and get my basketball. Want to come?" asked Lavell's friend Kevin.

"Sure," I said. It was nice to be singled out. And it seemed harmless. Kevin lived just a few blocks from the park.

We headed down the street and ended up at a house in a small addition behind a grocery store. Kevin left me on the front porch, while he went inside for the ball. Once he retrieved it, we started back to the park where my brother and the rest of his friends were hanging out. As we passed the grocery store, Kevin stopped. "Man I'm hungry—why don't you go get me one of those Hostess blueberry pies," he said.

"I would if I could Kevin, but I don't have any money."

"I don't care if you don't have any money. If you want to be my friend, you'll go get me a pie."

I knew better than to tell Kevin I was scared—it would only give my brother and their buddies one more thing to tease me about. Instead I told him I had never stolen anything before.

"If you want me to do it," I said, "you'll have to show me how."

He looked annoyed but started giving instructions.

"Go inside and find the pies. Wait until no one is looking and stick the pie down the front of your pants and walk out of the store," he said.

Kevin told me that he had done it many times before and he had never gotten caught. Kevin got his pie. And I didn't get caught, but being a fugitive didn't sit well with me either.

I don't think a day passed before I confessed to my grandpa.

"I'm disappointed in you Alton," he said. "There is no need for you to do things like that to impress people. A true friend would never ask you to prove yourself or do things that are illegal."

"But I don't have any friends," I said, "and I am tired of hanging out at home alone. I need something to do."

"Why don't you try and find a job?" Grandpa suggested. "Make a little spending money."

"That would be great, but who would hire me?"

"There are all kinds of things a boy your age could do," he said. "You could pick up aluminum cans around town and sell them to the recycle company down the street. Or maybe find some yards to mow. Goodness knows we have enough old mowers in the backyard, surely between them we can rig together one that'll run."

The mowing sounded more promising than picking up cans, though I felt Grandpa was a little optimistic about rehabbing one of his. His best mower was old and unreliable, and he often spent more time repairing it than he did mowing. But it was a race car compared to the ones hiding in the grass in the backyard. I was just about to give up the idea of my own lawn mowing business when Grandpa said, if I was willing to mow yards, he would buy me a mower.

It was the summer of 1980. He took me to a lawn-mower repair shop down the street and bought me an old used mower. It was green with half of the deck rusted out. None of the wheels matched, and the handle was bent as if it had been run over. She wasn't pretty but all I saw when I looked at that old rusty mower was a way to make some spending money.

We loaded my mower into the back of Grandpa's pickup and drove it home. When we got it unloaded, Grandpa gave me a small gas can (about half full of gasoline), showed me how to start and stop the mower, and told me I should go around the neighborhood and ask people if they needed their lawn mowed.

"Be polite," he said. "Even if they say, No."

With that, I headed out, pushing the mower from house to house, asking any neighbor who would come to the door, if they would be interested in letting me mow their yard.

Stepping out on my own like that was an act of faith. Most of the neighbors in a four-block radius did not know me personally by name, but many of them knew where I lived and that the police visited my grandparents' house regularly. So when I came knocking on their door asking if I could work for them, it did not surprise me when one after the other answered "no" without hesitation.

I went from house to house, up and down the street, and around the block getting rejected until I came to a little house on Arrington Street.

Chapter 16
Leona

The grass in the front yard of the little house was about a foot tall. It was questionable whether my old mower could even handle it, but I hoped that whoever lived there would give me a chance. So I pushed my mower up the driveway and knocked on the front door. A few seconds later, an elderly woman came to the door.

"Can I help you?" she asked.

"I'm trying to earn some money," I said, "and I was hoping you would hire me to mow your yard."

She looked me over, turned her eyes to my old mower sitting in the middle of her driveway, and then looked me over again.

"Come in and we'll talk about it," she said.

She escorted me into the dining room and had me take a seat at a small table with a white crocheted tablecloth. She excused herself and made her way to the kitchen, returning with a small glass of juice. She placed it in front of me on the table and then walked to the other side and sat down.

"What is your name?" she asked.

I told her my name and that I lived with my grandparents just around the corner, but I could tell by the look on her face that she knew all about my family. She told me her name was Leona Johnson, and that she had lived in the same house for many years, so she had seen a lot of people come and go in the neighborhood.

"How much would you charge to mow my lawn?" she asked.

I told her that honestly I had never mowed anyone's yard before, but I would mow hers for whatever she was willing to pay me. "My grandpa bought me the mower to help me earn some money," I said.

"I'll pay you seven dollars," she said, "and I have my own mower you can use, so you won't have to worry about buying gas. Come back this afternoon, and I'll put you to work."

I left her house with my first job. I pushed my old mower down the street back to my grandparents' house, eager to tell Grandpa about the elderly lady down the street who had hired me to mow her yard.

Then all I had to do was wait. The hours dragged by. When I finally convinced myself it was technically "later in the afternoon," I ran down the street and around the corner to Mrs. Johnson's house. I found her sitting on the porch waiting for me.

"I want you to call me, Leona," she told me. And when I protested, she insisted: "Alton, please, call me Leona."

That settled, I followed her through the garage to a small shed in the backyard. Just like the inside of Leona's house, the shed was clean and well kept with everything in its proper place. She spent the next few minutes showing me how to fuel and start her mower.

Leona was very particular and told me that while mowing, I should always push the mower forward because pulling the mower backwards could cause an injury to my feet. After she finished her instruction, I started the mower on the sidewalk like she had told me and began mowing the backyard. Leona stood watch on the back porch. The backyard done, I turned the mower off and headed around front, only to find Leona standing on the front porch holding a large glass of water with four or five ice cubes.

"Come take a break, Alton," she said. "I have some ice water for you."

I parked the mower in the front yard, and joined Leona on the porch. While I drank my ice water, Leona read her newspaper.

"Do you read the comics, Alton?" she asked after awhile.

"No, never," I said. "I don't like reading."

Leona moved her newspaper to the side and looked at me as though I had done something wrong.

"Why?" she asked.

"I'm not very good at it," I said.

"Reading is important Alton," she said. "You're going to need it your entire life. And the only way you're going to get better at reading is to read."

And then she said something I have never forgotten: "A person who can read and doesn't, is no better off than a person who can't read."

Before I could finish my ice water, Leona had it all figured out. She told me that from now on when I came to mow her lawn I had to read one newspaper article before starting work. I agreed without protest, but honestly I do not think she would have taken no for an answer. I have come to recognize that as a common denominator with Good Samaritans. Leona may not have found me on the side of the road and stopped to help, but she might as well have.

My break over, I finished mowing the front yard, then shut off the mower and parked it in the shed just the way Leona had shown me earlier. When I returned to the front yard, Leona was standing there with seven crisp one-dollar bills.

"The grass will be ready to mow again in two weeks," she said, as she handed over my pay.

With a big smile on my face, I took the money, thanked her, and ran all the way home to my grandparents'. I was so proud of what I had done. I had a job and was earning money, and it felt amazing.

My steps slowed only when I realized I could not tell anyone in my family I had the money because they would either take it or ask to borrow it with no intention of ever paying it back.

But by the time I reached my grandparents' house, all I could think about was what I was going to do with *my* seven dollars.

The Boy Who Carried Bricks

I think I'll go to the grocery store and buy myself something. I didn't know what I was going to buy, but surely I could find something once I got there. A few minutes later, I was standing in front of the grocery store I had been to so many times before for Grandma when she ran out of milk or sugar or eggs.

I went in and walked around for what seemed like hours, trying to decide what to buy. I really liked candy, so I made my way to the candy aisle and finally decided to purchase a six-pack of Snickers candy bars. I paid for my candy bars and set off back towards my grandparents' house.

Halfway through the park, I couldn't wait any longer. I headed for the bench near the swing set, opened my package of Snickers, unwrapped a bar, and took a bite. It was the best candy bar I had ever eaten, and each bite tasted better than the one before. I finished the first candy bar and opened another until I had eaten the entire pack.

For the rest of the summer, I went to Leona's house every two weeks, read a newspaper article, mowed her yard, and earned seven dollars. Between the front and backyard, she always insisted I take a break on the front porch while she read the paper.

As June turned to July and then August, she occasionally hired me to do other small tasks, changing light bulbs, sweeping out the garage, washing windows. And the last time I mowed her yard that summer instead of giving me a newspaper article to read, she gave me a brown hardback book that looked like it had been read many times before.

"I want you to take it home, read it, and then bring it back," she said.

As much as I had grown to like Leona, her gift was not welcomed. Reading was still a struggle for me, and I still hated it. Reading a newspaper was one thing; I had grown more confident in doing that. Reading a book was another thing entirely. Every time I had ever tried to read a book in the past, I had struggled not only to read but also to remember what I had read from page to page.

I took the book from her hands and read the title, *The Adventures of Huckleberry Finn.* Not only had I never heard of the book, I was also a ten-year-old who had never read a book from cover to cover. *What if I lose the book? What if I disappoint her because I can't finish it?*

Leona must have seen the fear in my eyes.

"I know you can read this book, Alton," she said. "It is just words on paper, like the newspaper articles you have read all summer. There is nothing to be scared about. I want you to take a month to read it, then bring it back so you can tell me all about it."

I took the book and read whenever I thought about it. It took me longer than a month to finish it, but when I did, I took the book back to Leona, and we spent an afternoon reliving the adventures of that rascal Huckleberry Finn.

As I talked about the story Leona's face lit up. I could tell she was proud of me, but it also felt like she was reading the book with me again. When I came to a part I couldn't quite remember, Leona would chime in and tell the adventure.

I hated to leave her that day, knowing it was the last time I would see her until the next mowing season. Funny, she lived right around the corner, but it never occurred to me she might want to see me outside of work.

For two summers I mowed for Leona Johnson, a little, old white lady who out of the kindness of her heart trusted me and allowed me to work for her while trying to instill in me a love of reading.

She cared about me when few others did. But even Leona's caring heart could not shield me from the wrath of my Uncle Stevie.

Chapter 17
Roaches & Gum

By sixth grade, I was staying with Mom as much as my grand-parents, despite what DHS had decreed. I had also developed a bad habit of talking back to my teachers and picking fights with other students. Several times a week I would be sent to the office. Mr. Mills, the middle-school principal, knew about my home life and did what he could to motivate me to follow the rules.

But I was caught up in what others had that I did not. I had reached that age where peer approval is everything, and clothes and how you looked mattered more than ever, especially when your wardrobe came used from the Salvation Army box or Goodwill store and everyone else's seemed to come new from a department store.

The first few times I found myself in the principal's office, Mr. Mills sat me down and tried to get me to share why I was so angry and making such poor choices. But when his talks did not alter my behavior, he moved on to corporeal punishment. I did not care for the swats much but not because they hurt. I had already endured at home far worse than a few hits with a wooden paddle. I just found them embarrassing.

Eventually, Mr. Mills figured out that corporeal punishment was not working and decided to move a desk into his office, just for me.

I missed lots of class time, and Mr. Mills had every right to suspend me from school but he never did, and I think it was because he knew what I had to go home to. I believe he knew that the best place for me was at school, even if it meant sitting in his office for most of the day. He had to have been frustrated at times, but he never gave up on me.

If he could have seen into my head, he would have learned that I left home hungry and came to school not carrying books but my family problems. I was mad because my mom was never around and neither was any food. We were lucky if we had electricity to help us see our way around the house at night. When we did have electricity, turning on the lights made the roaches scurry for cover. When we had cereal, it was quickly rendered inedible, because the bugs took up house in the box.

The roach infestation got so bad they often came to school with me, crawling out of my clothes during class. It was mortifying. Everyone knew the source of the bugs. It became an embarrassing routine: Someone would spot a roach, point at it and then me, and the class would erupt in laughter.

"Grossssss Alton," someone would say.

"You have bugs coming out of your clothes," someone else would chime in.

The teachers never seemed to know how to handle the situation. My next stop was usually the principal's office.

*****

I was not acting any better at home. I had discovered where Mom hid the food stamps, and decided I was going to steal some to buy me something at the store. That was my plan. I took twenty dollars worth of stamps from under her mattress and set out.

As hungry as I always was, you'd have thought I would have bought a burrito or a box of cookies that day. I ended up buying a package of Hubba Bubba chewing gum. And instead of keeping it for myself I took it to school and sold it to my classmates during recess. Everybody chewed gum during recess so I knew I would have plenty of customers. The first day, I only sold a few packs and made just a few dollars. But I was optimistic sales would improve.

Within a few weeks, I was selling out of gum before recess was over. I used the money I made to buy snacks at the neighborhood gas station, though I must say they never went down all that well. Guilt makes a lousy condiment. And I felt guilty for essentially stealing money from my mom.

I knew eventually Mom would discover her food stamps were missing and figure out it was me who had taken them, so one day I just came clean with her. I don't remember getting in trouble for my gum-selling scam. If anything Mom must have condoned it, because from then on, my gum profits went to help her pay the bills and buy groceries.

It was still wrong but it did feel good to help out the family, and though Mom never told me, I could tell she really appreciated it.

Chapter 18
Lowering the Broom

Uncle Stevie's moods changed as quickly and as frequently as the Oklahoma weather. No one ever knew what mood Uncle Stevie would be in when he came home at night. Some evenings he made us wrestle for his entertainment; other nights he commandeered the TV. On this particular night, however, our grandparents' living room had become a fight club.

I was paired with my little brother, Dejohn, and he was getting the best of me. I was bigger and stronger than Dejohn, but he was tougher and meaner. At one point in our match, Dejohn had me in a headlock and pinned to the ground. I tried everything to get loose, but was unable to get free.

Standing over us like a coach, Uncle Stevie shouted instructions to Dejohn on how to hurt me even more—both mentally and physically. "Come on Dejohn, you're tougher than he is; you're dominating him. Finish the sissy off."

Already embarrassed about getting pinned by my little brother, I did the one thing that could make my situation even worse: I started crying. Uncle Stevie went ballistic.

"You better stop crying Alton—be a man," he yelled.

But the more he yelled at me, the more I cried. Finally Uncle Stevie had had enough.

"If you don't stop your crying, Alton, I'm going to get the broom and give you something to cry about. You got to stop being such a crybaby and learn to fight, like a man, or everyone at school is gonna beat you up."

As Uncle Stevie leaned over me with his finger in my face yelling, I did not dare move, too afraid of what he might do next.

"Go get the broom from the kitchen, Dejohn."

Dejohn hustled out of the room, and my uncle turned back to me. "I'm going to give you one last chance," he said. "If you don't stop crying like a little girl by the time Dejohn comes back with that broom, I'm going to beat you with it."

He let me ponder his threat.

Sure enough Dejohn returned with the broom, and I was still crying. Uncle Stevie snatched the broom out of Dejohn's hand, raised it over his head, and bellowed: "I told you to stop crying, Alton!"

I took one look at him and, without thinking, took off running towards the stairs that led downstairs to my grandparents' bedroom. I had gone only a few feet when I felt the broom strike the top of my head.

Crack!

I fell to the floor with Stevie looming over me, half of a broom handle still in his hand. The other half was on the floor beside me. I must have made some noise when I hit the floor because my grandpa started yelling.

"What's going on up there," Grandpa shouted.

Dizzy, unable to stand, I couldn't answer my grandpa for fear of what my uncle might do next.

"I said, 'What's going on?' " Grandpa hollered again.

This time I could tell he was at the bottom of the staircase. No one said a word. I didn't dare; Dejohn and the others were not about to cross Uncle Stevie; and goodness knows Uncle Stevie was not about to rat out himself. Eventually when no one would answer, Grandpa gave up and returned to his room. I managed to crawl to the nearest couch, while Uncle Stevie explained to my siblings and cousins how much of a baby I was. Maybe he was right, but it was not something I was willing to change.

I found it easier to run when fights started than to stand and fight like other boys. Hurting others to prove how tough I was never appealed to me.

*****

Like most people, Uncle Stevie was not all bad, all the time. When he wasn't drinking, he could actually be quite fun. Some nights he would tiptoe into the living room where all of us kids slept and whisper, "You guys awake?"

All seven of us would almost always sit up at the same time and reply, "Yes, Uncle Stevie, we're awake." We knew what was coming.

"Well good, if you're all awake and can be quiet, I will tell you a story," he would say.

Seven heads would solemnly nod. And Uncle Stevie would start spinning one of his tales. He concocted them out of thin air, but we enjoyed them all the same. Sometimes, his stories were scary, and we would cover our heads with our blankets and cower with fear. Most nights, our uncle followed his storytelling by making a fresh batch of homemade French fries.

His tall tales over, Uncle Stevie would lead us into the kitchen to make the fries. And all seven of us would tiptoe after him, quiet as mice, knowing there was one more hurdle we had to cross before we could enjoy what we believed were the best fries in the entire world.

The challenge? Not to scream when the kitchen light came on.

We did not want to wake Grandma and Grandpa or the other uncles, as doing so would have at the very least ended our unexpected midnight snack. And, as I have said before, we were always hungry. But not screaming took incredible self-control for seven little kids. You see, flipping the light switch on sent roaches scattering this way and that—and sometimes wayward bugs would fall off the ceiling and land on someone, which always produced a scream.

We were used to roaches in the daytime, because they were constantly in the fridge, the cabinets, and the sink full of dirty dishes from days gone by. In fact, most days if we were quiet and listened, we could actually hear roaches crawling all over our kitchen . . . and, sometimes, each other. At least once a month, one of us kids had to be taken to the doctor to get roaches removed from our ears.

But despite roaches being an everyday bane of our existence, we never quite got over the shock of seeing the floor turn into thousands of scurrying roaches when that light came on.

The nights we managed to hold our screams, we got our reward, as Uncle Stevie scraped out the leftover food and roaches from Grandma's cast iron skillet, peeled potatoes, filled the skillet with grease, and fried his trademark potatoes.

If only every night with Uncle Stevie could have been like that.

*****

The nights when Uncle Stevie got drunk it was hard to remember the uncle who made French fries. Drunk Uncle Stevie was a mean and punishing man, always on the lookout for someone to hurt, usually one of us. Thankfully most of the time we could smell the alcohol before he fumbled his way into the house.

With whiskey bottle in hand, our uncle would stumble his way into the living room, screaming, "are you b------- awake?" We knew better than to respond; instead we lay so still under our blankets you would have thought we were dead. But when Uncle Stevie had an itch, you could bet he intended to scratch it.

On would come the lights as he kicked us out of our various spots on the floor. To the couch he would send us, lining us up side by side with a threat not to move or utter a sound or else. Into the kitchen he then went for a cup, then back to the couch where we still sat. One by one he then forced us to share his whiskey: "Drink it, and if any of you tells anyone about this, I'll kill you."

His request and threat rarely varied, but they never lost their impact on us. We had seen Uncle Stevie fistfight with his brothers, and we had watched him beat his girlfriends with both his fists and his belt. We all knew his words were not a threat.

They were a promise, so we did what he asked, without question. We drank.

And then the next day we struggled to hide our hangovers and queasy tummies from our grandparents.

Chapter 19
Stories & French Fries

The nights not spent listening to his stories, eating French fries, drinking Uncle Stevie's whiskey, or playing The Wishing Game, we spent on the street helping my uncle scam people. That was how he financed his drinking.

Uncle Stevie would load all seven cousins into his car, take us to one of the town's busiest streets, and park on the side of the road with the hood up to make it appear we were broken down. When someone stopped to assist us, he would send one of the cousins to tell the motorist we had run out of fuel and needed money for gas. Most people gave us money. How could they turn their back on a man stranded on the side of the road with seven kids?

If our Good Samaritans insisted on going to the gas station to purchase the fuel, Uncle Stevie would send one of us kids with them. More times than not, we came back with snacks for everyone and gas for the car. It was a win-win situation anyway it played out.

Uncle Stevie's car was faded brown with chipped paint and a cracked back window. The rear end was smashed, and the trunk required a hanger tied to the bumper to keep it closed. The radio was missing, and cigarette burns dotted the worn seats. People would take one look at the car and all the children, and they were fooled instantly.

Another one of Uncle Stevie's favorite targets were Salvation Army boxes. Shaped like a little red house, the boxes stood about six feet tall with a swinging door in the top front so people could deposit donations of unwanted household items and old clothes. You could find the boxes in almost every grocery store parking lot in our town.

Uncle Stevie's scam called for him to pull his car up to a box, shove one of the cousins through the swinging door, and then hand in a flashlight so we could look for anything of value. Whatever items we found, Uncle Stevie would later pawn to buy his whiskey.

The scam usually went off without a hitch, but on one of my turns in the box the police pulled up and started questioning Uncle Stevie about what he was doing there. I watched the whole conversation unfold through a crack.

"I'm just making a donation, officers," Uncle Stevie said.

"Really," the officer said. "So what did you donate?"

Uncle Stevie, usually so smooth and glib, froze as the officer walked over to the Salvation Army box and pushed the swinging door open with his flashlight only to find me wide-eyed and looking up at him. The officer quickly pulled me out of the box and told me to get into Uncle Stevie's car.

"I have every right to take you to jail," the officer then told Uncle Stevie. "But I won't, so long as you promise not to ever do this again."

It was a victory for our uncle, and a loss for us. How I wished our uncle had gone to jail that night. I wanted so badly to tell the cops about Uncle Stevie and the things he did to us. I wanted to scream for their help, but I lacked the nerve.

What will happen if the police don't believe me, I thought. The fear of being left to face Uncle Stevie after telling on him kept me silent, and I watched my hopes drive away with the police car.

As we drove back to my grandparents' that night, I knew I had to do something. I could not take his abuse anymore. I had to stand up for myself. I decided no matter what Uncle Stevie threatened to

do to me, I was not drinking any more of his whiskey. What I was not prepared to do, however, was to have to back up my vow that very same night.

As we piled out of the car, I saw my uncle reach in the glove compartment and pull out a brown paper sack. My heart sunk because I knew what was inside.

In the house, Uncle Stevie went straight to the kitchen and brought out a sixteen-ounce cup. With cup in one hand and bottle in the other, he directed us to line up on the couch and held out the booze. One by one my siblings and cousins took their turn drinking the whiskey. But when the cup was handed to me, I shook my head—all the while looking at the floor.

With my head down and my eyes on the floor, I heard my brother say, "Drink it Alton." I refused again with a shake of my head. I had Uncle Stevie's attention now. With his whiskey bottle in his hand, he moved until he stood before me, a dark tower of anger.

"Drink the whiskey Alton, or I'm going to give you a beating you won't soon forget."

I will never know where the courage came from, but I stood up, so close to him I could smell his whiskey breath when he exhaled, and looked him in the eye: "I don't care what you do to me, Uncle Stevie, I am not drinking that anymore."

For a moment, the room was dead silent. I realized what happened next would change my life forever. His face shifted from shock to rage. His fists closed, as though he was about to punch me. He threw his whiskey down on the filthy, stained carpet, and with his left hand under my right arm and his right hand near my left calf, he picked me up in the air and began walking across the room.

I was high enough in the air that as he moved toward the front door, I could look down and make eye contact with my younger brothers whose eyes were filled with fear and sympathy.

Just short of the door, Uncle Stevie stopped, turned to his right, and threw me down the stairs. I rolled as if I had fallen out of a moving car into a ditch. I landed on my back, just in time to see him running down the stairs after me. For a moment I thought he had realized what he had done and was coming to see if I was okay, but I was wrong. When my uncle reached the bottom of the stairs, instead of offering me a hand he started kicking me. After a few hard kicks to my rib cage, I somehow managed to escape down the hall to where my grandparents slept.

I didn't say a word to them, and I remember wondering how they could sleep through all the noise. But I didn't wake them. Instead, I grabbed the phone off the night table on my grandma's side of the bed. When I lifted the receiver, the lights on the phone lit up the dark room, and I could see clearly to dial 9-1-1.

"9-1-1 what's your emergency."

"He's trying to kill me!" I screamed.

With that, I dropped the phone and ran from the room, back down the hallway to the back of the house. I expected to find Uncle Stevie waiting for me in the hallway, but he was nowhere to be seen. Still I wasn't taking any chances. I fled out the backdoor and hid behind our neighbor's car and waited for what seem like an eternity until I saw the flashing red and blue lights coming over the hill.

When the police car was about a block away, I ran out in the middle of the street—jumping up and down pointing towards my grandparents' house.

Within minutes, several police cars, all with their lights flashing, were parked in front of our house, lighting up the neighborhood like it was Christmas. I stood in the middle of the street, crying and terrified; I explained to two of the police officers what had happened and showed them the bumps on my head from my fall and the bruises on my side where my uncle had kicked me.

The officers conferred for a moment with another policeman, and then one stayed with me and the other two headed for our front door. Before they could knock, however, my grandma opened the door and began telling them that everything was fine and they needed to leave.

The officers tried to explain to her that they couldn't leave because a crime had been committed, and that she needed to send Stevie to the front door. She refused and began to yell profanities at the officers. With that, the officers shoved Grandma aside and entered the house. A few minutes later, they exited with Uncle Stevie in handcuffs and put him in back of one of the police cars.

By now, all the cousins were standing behind Grandma while the officer tried once more to tell her why they were there and why her son was going to jail. Grandma didn't like it, I could tell, but there was nothing she could do this time.

One by one, the officers got in their cars and drove off. The last car to leave had my uncle in the back, but I was afraid to look because I could feel him staring at me. I was also starting to worry about what Grandma might have to say to me.

I went looking for my grandpa—I knew if anyone would support me in what I had done that it would be him—but he was nowhere to be found.

I headed upstairs to the sound of my grandmother calling me, "Snitch. Narc. And Uncle Tom." My siblings and cousins joined in.

"How could you do it, Alton," one asked. "How could you do that to your own family?"

"How could you call the cops on Uncle Stevie?" another said.

I understood Grandma turning a blind eye to the doings of her sons, but I will never understand what possessed my brothers and sister and cousins to turn on me. They knew what Uncle Stevie was like. I wasn't the only one he had hurt. They should have been thanking me, but instead I felt alone and almost ashamed of what I had done.

I didn't feel as though I belonged there anymore. So I turned around and walked back down the stairs and out of the house, though I had nowhere to go.

Chapter 20
Night in the Park

My only friend lived nearly twelve miles outside of town. Tim's mother would have come and gotten me nonetheless, but I had no way to call her. So I walked over to the park and found a bench while I tried to figure out what to do.

Eventually, I crawled into the big covered slide and fell fast asleep. The next morning, I woke up knowing I could not go back to my grandparents' house. Having crossed one of her sons, Grandma would not want me around anymore, and I knew it would be just a matter of time before she bailed Uncle Stevie out of jail. Going back to her house would mean facing Uncle Stevie and living the nightmare all over again. I just couldn't do it.

Truth be told, it wasn't Uncle Stevie's beatings that bothered me. I'd grown used to them. It was the alcohol, the stealing, and the nights on the streets running scams for him that I could not take. Doing such things made me feel dirty and ashamed.

That morning I made the decision that I would never live with my family again. I wanted to be different; I wanted to be normal— I wanted to do the right thing and to have nice things. I wanted a chance to succeed and to be respected, and I knew if I returned home, I would become like them. So I walked right past my grandparents' house, headed to the Department of Human Services office. I had plenty of time to think about what I was doing on my three-mile walk. Before I even got to where I was going, I was already feeling guilty about leaving my family but I was also wondering where DHS would send me.

Once I got there, the process took over. I explained what had happened the night before to a caseworker, and she called the police to confirm my story. My story confirmed, she asked if there was anyone I could live with, and immediately I thought about my friend Tim. I told the caseworker I had a good friend with whom I often stayed when I needed to get away from things at home.

Tim's mom, Barbara, was recently divorced with joint custody of her three, adopted kids. She worked at the university as a college academic adviser; she knew about my home life, but never judged me and had always treated me as though I was one of her own children. Her ex-husband, however, was a child psychologist and not particularly fond of either my family or me. Still it was worth a try.

The caseworker called and asked Tim's mom if I could stay with them with hopes that I might even live there permanently. Barbara was all for it, but she needed the approval of her ex-husband and to run it by her own children.

Meanwhile, I went to the youth shelter. A few days later, Barbara and the caseworker showed up at the shelter, and I was asked to join them in one of the meeting rooms. Though I had known moving in with Tim and his mom was a long shot, I just felt in my gut I was about to get good news, but I was wrong.

"I would love to have you come stay with us," Barbara said, "but my ex-husband says if you do, he will take my children away from me. I am so sorry."

With tears in her eyes, she told me she loved me and no matter where I went, I could always come and visit. Then she gave me a hug and was gone.

Chapter 21
Rader

My options exhausted, my DHS caseworker assigned me to a high security juvenile detention center east of Stillwater called Lloyd E. Rader. Rader was extremely large, and from the outside looked like a prison. The facility had eight to ten buildings enclosed by a ten-foot, chain-link fence topped with barbed wire.

Entering the place was like entering a prison complete with a security gate. IDs had to be checked and identities confirmed. My caseworker and I met with the director who assigned me to one of the buildings; there we met two unfriendly counselors who went through all my bags, checking for contraband. Not much for small talk, they kept our conversation limited to the center's rules and expectations followed by a list of punishments for youngsters breaking said rules. It was 1981. I was eleven years old.

The rules were about what one would expect to find in such a place: no drinking or smoking, no fighting or being disrespectful to other kids or counselors, doing your chores. The punishment for breaking the rules, however, seemed strange. Along with privileges being taken away for breaking a rule, you could also be put in the

Time Out Room, a seven-by-ten-foot room outfitted with only a toilet, a metal bed, a single metal door, and a one-by-one-foot window. The room itself was made of cement bricks. They called it being put in TOR.

Our living quarters were spare and functional. Girls and boys were housed apart. My area had about ten beds, separated by short three-foot brick walls to provide some privacy while still allowing the counselors to be able to see us at all times.

It all made me uneasy, but it wasn't until I met some of the other kids that I wondered how I had ended up in a place like this. One boy told me he was there because he had tried to kill his parents. His graphic description of how he had tied his parents up and tried to stab them to death left me confused and terrified. And then there was the quiet but beautiful blonde girl with the green eyes who never spoke to anyone. I had noticed the scars on her wrists, and so I thought she might be at Rader for cutting or trying to kill herself, but then one day, she and another girl got into an argument while standing in line for lunch. The blonde girl became so upset she started pummeling the other girl with her fists until the girl fell to the ground. It took two adult counselors to subdue the blonde girl, and they had to carry her out in a white straight jacket—all the while she was screaming at the top of her lungs.

I heard later they took her to TOR where she continued to scream for hours for someone to free her. Every fifteen minutes or so, a counselor would check on her through the tiny window. This went on the entire day and into the evening. A counselor had to feed her dinner by hand that night, because they didn't dare remove the straight jacket for fear of what she might do to herself or someone else.

The next morning it was quiet again, so I figured they had moved her out of TOR and back to her room. But I learned at breakfast that it was quiet because the blonde girl had left in the middle of the night. It took me a while, but I finally got over the fact that I had never summoned the courage to say a word to the blonde girl.

Chapter 22
Christmas

The drama surrounding the blonde girl's disappearance helped me keep my mind off the fact that Christmas was just around the corner. It was always a bittersweet time for me. You couldn't help getting caught up in the magic of the holiday, but the holiday played itself out very differently at our home.

I had counted on the fact that I would not get a gift from my family, but I had hoped my mom or my grandparents would come see me during the two-hour family Christmas visit we were allowed.

Visiting day arrived, and the counselors explained that each visiting family would be escorted to the kitchen, and the name of the child they were there to see would be called. We could then go outside or sit in the common area to visit.

I was a nervous wreck because I hadn't seen or talked to my family in months. I worried they might still be mad at me for getting Uncle Stevie thrown in jail. I was afraid they might come just to tell me how terrible I was for calling the police on him.

One by one names were called, and my peers got up and joined their families until I was the only one left.

I sat there, all by myself, doing the math. Stillwater was only forty minutes away from Sand Springs, so surely someone was coming to see me. But the hours ticked away and my name was never called. When I couldn't take it anymore, I got up and went to my room where I spent the rest of the day. We were generally not allowed in our rooms except to sleep, but I think the counselors must have felt sorry for me because this time no one said a word.

For the next couple of days, I moped. Truth be told, I was more disappointed in myself for thinking my family would come than I was about them not showing up. Their absence just confirmed what I already knew: I didn't want to grow up and be like them.

A few days later, one of the counselors brought me a small package wrapped in brown paper. "Merry Christmas, Alton" was written across the front. I ripped it open and found a watch inside, with a note that read:

> Dear Alton,
> I am sorry that I missed your Christmas visit.
> I hope you enjoy this watch. Merry Christmas!
> Love, Mom

I pulled the watch out of the case and put it on my wrist as fast as I could. I knew Mom never had any money (most Christmases we received one small gift from our grandparents or nothing), so the watch could not have been worth much, but I didn't care. *I am going to wear this watch forever and only take it off when I shower.*

And that is exactly what I did. I wore that watch every day and showed it to everyone and anyone who would take a look. It had been a long time since I had owned something of which I could be proud. But Rader was not the place for wearing or having nice things. And one afternoon while playing cards in the common area, an older boy approached me.

"I want your watch," he said, looking me straight in the eye.

"No," I said without even thinking. "My mom gave me this watch. It's not worth much, but it is the only thing I have from her."

"Give me the watch or I'll punch you in the face," the boy said.

"No," I said.

This same exchange repeated itself for several days. Every day the boy told me if I didn't give him my watch he was going to hit me. Every day I told him, No—until one day before I could move or defend myself, the boy drew back his arm, balled up his fist, and punched me right in my left eye. Before he walked away, he told me he would be back to ask again tomorrow, and if I didn't give up my watch then, I could expect to be punched again.

And he was a man of his word. The next day during lunch he came up and asked me for my watch.

"No," I said, just like the day before and the day before that.

Once again the boy drew back his arm, clenched his fist, and hit me, this time in my nose and left eye.

For several days, this became our routine. But I told myself that no matter how hard he hit me, I would not give up my watch. I knew if I gave up my watch to him today, tomorrow he would ask for something else. So I had made up my mind that he was not getting my watch no matter how many times he hit me.

Sure enough, one day the boy didn't drop by at lunch. From then on, he left me alone.

And I felt better for having stood up for myself.

I stayed at Rader for several more weeks before being picked up by my caseworker and taken back to the youth shelter in Stillwater.

Chapter 23
The Boys Ranch

I was only back at the Stillwater youth shelter for a few days when my caseworker told me she was taking me to the Oklahoma Lions Boys Ranch in Perkins, Oklahoma, about fifteen minutes south of home. I left the shelter in 1982 with mixed emotions. I was still worried about my siblings, especially with Uncle Stevie back at Grandma's, but I knew I had to leave Stillwater if I wanted a fighting chance at a better life.

Perkins is a typical rural Oklahoma community: Lots of cowboy hats and boots. Lots of trucks with gun racks hanging in the rear windows. The boys ranch sat surrounded by pastures a few miles outside of town, on the other side of the muddy red waters of the Cimarron River.

A long, single-story, white house with an unusual roof shaped like a wavy cloud, the ranch house had a pasture with forty head of cattle and several other small houses instead of a front yard. To the left of the pasture were the pigpens, which held twenty or so pigs. Directly to the left of the house was another large pen that held fifteen sheep. I had arrived at what looked to be a real working ranch.

The Boy Who Carried Bricks

Our ranch parents were Bert and Bee Baits. Brown-haired and balding, Bert was slightly chunky and stood about five-foot-six, and from the moment I met him, I could tell he suffered from Short Man's Syndrome. Bee was a quiet petite woman who tended to stand behind Bert and let him do all the talking.

The Baitses gave us a quick tour of the house. The living room and kitchen looked like what you would find in any other house, but the hallway where the bedrooms and bathrooms were, looked more like a prison cellblock. Seven bedrooms lined one side of the long hallway with the bathrooms and laundry on the other. At the end of the hallway, a single locked door separated us from the ranch parents' bedroom.

I did not mind how much the place looked like a prison, and I sure did not mind the Ranch parents locking themselves in their room at night, away from us. I was just excited about what lay ahead for me at the ranch. Despite all the disappointments thus far in my young life, I never lost hope that a new day might bring a better life.

The tour of the ranch over, my DHS caseworker said her good-byes and left me in the care of the Baitses. She had no more driven out of sight, than Bert sat me down and explained there were a few rules he had failed to mention before.

Overlooked Rule Number One: Every boy at the ranch calls the Baitses, Mom and Dad.

"You will, too," he said.

Bert said he knew doing so could take a little getting used to, so he would give me a few weeks to adjust. I had never called anyone "Dad." And it seemed odd to call Bee "Mom," when I had a very much alive mother of my own back home in Stillwater. But I didn't protest. I could tell Bert was just getting started.

"Any time I call your name or speak to you, you are to reply, 'Yes, sir' or 'No, sir,' and whenever Bee calls you, you are to answer 'Yes, ma'am' or 'No, ma'am.'

"Daily chores—washing dishes, cleaning the bathrooms—will be assigned every Monday, and the list posted on the bulletin board in the hallway.

"Meals will be at the same time each day. Bee rings a bell to let us know when meals are ready. Once the bell is rung, you have ten minutes to wash up and be standing behind your assigned chair at the table. All four legs of your chair are to stay on the floor. If you spill a beverage, you will go one week without anything to drink during meals."

He told me that church was important, and because he was a deacon at a church in Stillwater we would all be in that church Sunday mornings at nine, Sunday evenings at six, and Wednesday evenings at six.

"You boys all sit together on the front row, and there is no goofing off or talking during the service," he said.

I would be given a notebook and pencil that I was to use to take notes at the ranch, church, and school. There would be random inspection of our notebooks, and if Bert found I was not taking notes properly, I would be disciplined.

Attending school was a must, and he told me he expected me to make good grades. Homework was to be completed as soon as I got home from school. If at anytime I had a D in school, I would run two miles, three days a week until my grade was raised to a C. If I made an F in school, I would run two miles, five days a week until I raised it up to a C, and if at any time I had more than one bad grade, I would run seven days a week.

There were two ways to run: laps around the ranch house or what he called "a trip to the office." The office was a building about a mile down the road from the ranch. If I was told to run to the office, I would have to run to the office and back in a designated length of time. If I didn't make the time, I would have to run again.

Room inspections were done at random so my room was to be clean at all times. I was not to hang any pictures or posters on the wall. My bed was to be made as soon as I got out of it in the morning, and I was not to leave my room until my bed was made. Dirty clothes went in my clothes hamper, never on the floor.

Since all the boys at the ranch wore the same white T-shirts and blue jeans, I would be given a marker to put my initials on every piece of my clothing. Bee washed and folded our clothes on Saturdays and Wednesdays, and having my initials on my garments would help her keep them together. I could pick my clothes up in the laundry room after they were washed. Clean clothes had to be removed from the laundry on Saturdays and Wednesdays before bedtime. All jeans and dress shirts were to be hung on hangers; all other clothes were to be stacked on the shelves in our door-less closets.

Every boy at the ranch also had to memorize the IOA Boys Creed before he got his first group ranking of Tenderfoot. The creed went like this:

"I" for Individual, with spark divine ("Myself at my Best");

"O" for Opportunity, or a life that's fine ("Learning as I Earn");

"A" for Achievement, which comes from sharing mine!

("Growing Up" in Body, Mind, and Soul . . . My attitude at Home, at School, at Church, and in the Community . . . at Work, at Prayer . . .

I'll be a Helping Hand as I follow the "I-O-A" Trail from "Champ-Nit" to "Champion" . . .

I'll learn Ben Franklin's 5-Step Formula to Solving Difficult Problems . . . and how to measure My Growth as I become a Champion.)

Rank brought with it perks. There were three levels: Tenderfoot, Hand, and Top Hand. The rank of Tenderfoot would allow me to play sports, receive a $1.25 monthly allowance, and have a 9:30 p.m. curfew. The rank of Hand would allow me to watch television on Saturdays, receive a $2.50 monthly allowance, and have a 10 p.m.

curfew. The rank of Top Hand would allow me to receive a $4.25 monthly allowance, have a 10:30 p.m. curfew, and have the option to own and drive a car when I turned sixteen.

After going over the long list of rules and chores, Bert had one last warning: "You break any rule or commit any violation, and I deal with it as I see fit. You want to survive here, you pull your weight and do what you're told."

With that said, he took me to the room I would occupy during my three years at the ranch. It was nothing special but had the bare necessities. It didn't matter to me; I was just glad to have a room of my own.

I was more worried about all of Bert's rules, though part of me couldn't help wondering if maybe this is what constituted "normal life" for other people. Somehow I didn't think so. My gut told me there was more to his rules than Bert had explained to me.

Looking back, almost every boy at the ranch received his Tenderfoot promotion but only a very few were promoted to Hand. During my time at the boys ranch, we were rarely allowed to watch TV and only two of us ever made Top Hand. We were, in fact, kids held hostage in the country by an evil obsessive man who claimed to be a Christian doing God's work, by saving troubled boys.

In fact, nothing could have been farther from the truth.

Chapter 24
Carrying Bricks

Hauling hay was a big part of summer at the boys ranch. We hauled hay from dawn to dinner. Bee would fill a cooler of water and make each boy two sandwiches to take with us to the fields. Bert told us we sold the hay to raise money to help support the ranch. For every bale of hay sold, each boy received one penny—the rest went to the ranch fund.

In the winter we cut trees for firewood. That was our winter crop to sell. Bert had us load the chain saws, axes, and fuel in the truck bed, and then we would cut through the pasture where the cattle were usually kept and head for the river down an old beaten path.

We stopped wherever Bert saw fit and went to work. Bert would fire up the chain saw and begin cutting down trees. Our job was to stay out of the way while clearing away the small limbs as he lopped them off the tree.

Once we had a pile of small limbs, one of us boys would start a fire to burn the brush. The only two rules while cutting trees with Bert was to never get caught standing around and to remove the limbs as soon as he cut them.

Bert was a hard worker, and he taught us the value of hard honest labor. It was important to him that we learned to take pride in everything we did.

Once Bert cut away all the small limbs from the tree, he began cutting the trunk and larger branches into sixteen-inch logs. One boy was assigned to split the logs, while two others stacked the split wood in the truck.

It didn't take long for us to become a well-oiled machine. Every boy had an assigned job until it was time to take a break. We usually worked about four hours cutting, burning, splitting, and carrying wood.

Once the truck bed was full of logs, Bert would tell us to follow him back up to the house. We walked behind the truck the half-mile back to the house, and then went to work stacking the wood on the front porch or near the barn.

On days Bert was mad at us, instead of hauling the wood up from the river in the truck, he would make us carry it by hand. Each boy would make eight to ten round-trips from the place we cut wood to the two places we stacked it.

Come to find out, hauling wood was good practice for what Bert had in store for some of us. The man was a taskmaster, and he believed in the power of punishment. I still marvel at some of the punishments he handed down.

His go-to-punishment was running laps. The number around the house might vary from twelve to seventy-two. Bert handed this punishment down for almost anything we did wrong. If our bedroom didn't pass inspection, we had to run laps. If we didn't work hard enough, we had to run laps. We were required to always wear a belt and have our shirts tucked in, so any time we forgot our belt or didn't tuck our shirt in, we had to run laps.

One of his more original punishments was carrying bricks. If you were told to carry bricks, you did it in two-hour increments, and your job was to carry five bricks the sixty yards from one side of the yard to the other, set each brick down in a stack, one on top of the other, and return for another five, and repeat until your time was up.

The Boy Who Carried Bricks

To keep anyone from loafing, Bert had a certain number of bricks that had to be moved in any given two-hour span or you had to go again. This was often a solo form of punishment, but sometimes if a group of us made Bert mad he would have us all carry bricks. Carrying bricks wasn't about correcting bad behavior or building character; it was about torture, pure and simple.

Bert also liked his bear crawls, a punishment that was handed down every single day to at least someone—and, like carrying the bricks, often the whole group.

Bear crawls involved doing laps on all fours, basically on our hands and feet. Every time we passed the front door, we had to call out the number of laps completed. On average we crawled no less than six laps, but on a few occasions I saw boys do as many as eighteen. And if Bert were really upset with you, he would walk behind and kick you in the rear every time you stopped to take a break or your knees touched the ground.

One afternoon we were mending fences about a half-mile away from the ranch house, and Bert got mad and told us he was tired of us all being so lazy and that we needed to be taught a lesson.

"Bear crawl back to the house," he ordered.

And so we did, on all fours all the way back to the house with him driving behind us in his truck.

Bear crawling that half-mile felt more like three hundred, and crawling through the rough grass cut our palms, but that pain could not compare to the pain we felt in our arms and backs. Not only did we have to avoid holes and small trees, but we were constantly encountering cow patties in the pasture. In some places, the grass was so tall that we couldn't even see each other. At other times, sweat poured off our heads so fast we couldn't see through the wet.

If anyone dared stop or stand up, Bert would yell, but there wasn't a lot he could do to make us keep going when our arms were shaking, buckling, and cramping, and our backs were giving out. Our leg muscles burned so hot they felt as though they were on fire.

No matter how bad our bodies hurt, however, we knew we had to make it back to the house or face an even worse punishment. So we urged each other on, and if one of us seemed like he was about to give up, someone would bear crawl beside him until he started to believe he could go on again.

Bert didn't schedule any rest stops for our crawl, but we decided as a group that when one of us needed to rest we would all stop, that way he couldn't single out just one of us to yell at or punish.

Each of us boys was at the ranch for a different reason. Some had come to the ranch to avoid going to a lockdown juvenile facility. Others were there because they had been physically abused, and more than a few were there because they had no family to take care of them. We were a wary bunch, not prone to easily make friends, but crawling in that pasture that day built an amazing bond between us that even Bert's cruelty couldn't break.

Our bond was built not on friendship but more the camaraderie of war—we were only as strong as our weakest link; it certainly wasn't built on respect for Bert, but rather on a mutual hatred we harbored against this man who dared call himself a Christian.

Chapter 25
Deacon Bert

My family had never been regular churchgoers, but I had been to church more than a few times in my life, and the church where Bert was a deacon was like no church I had ever seen.

Every Sunday, Bert and Bee drove us all into town in the ranch van for the service. Bert made us walk into church single file—dressed in our church slacks and dress shirts—and sit in the front row. Every time I walked into that church, I felt less and less like a child of God.

It always felt like the congregation was staring at us like we were demon-possessed boys in need of saving. They rarely spoke to us but greeted Bert as though he were an angel charged with an important task. I blamed some of their confusion on the preacher, who specialized in fire-and-brimstone sermons and was known to play records backward, claiming their lyrics contained messages from the devil. That man talked a good game, but I never felt God's love in his church.

Going to that church brought on a whole new batch of issues that I needed resolved. Problem was, the more we went to church with Bert the more I wondered if God could see what I was going through at the ranch—thanks to Bert. I wanted to ask the preacher or someone who might know if God could see me, but I never got the chance, so late one night I wrote my questions down in a poem.

Can He See Me

(Young Alton)
Can you tell me, sir
If God can hear me cry?
When my tears start to fall
Will He know the reason why?
Does He know I am hurting?
Can He see that I'm in pain?
Will He love me as I am,
As my tears fall like rain?

(Preacher)
Yes, I know the answer
It's easy you will see
He loves you very much
He died for you and me.

I never got a chance to ask the preacher those questions, and I'm glad. I suspect his answer would have been quite different than my poem. I say this, because every Sunday he looked over his pulpit he would have had to be a blind man not to see the pain and hurt in our eyes, yet he said nothing and did nothing to ease our burden. I don't remember him once visiting the ranch.

As for Bert, blind obedience is what he was all about. It was important to move quickly whenever he asked you to do anything because if you didn't, he would make you do bear crawls or run laps.

One Saturday after we had finished our usual chores, Bert assigned each of us an outside chore. The tasks ranged from cleaning the pigpen to clearing out the barn. I drew helping Bert change the oil in the tractor. Given to us by a donor, we used the tractor for cutting the grass and hauling hay. Bert was religious about keeping it serviced.

Bert crawled under the tractor and told me to run to the barn and bring back his toolbox. I did as I was told. Bert grabbed the wrench he needed and removed the oil pan. He handed the oil pan to me and told me to clean it while he finished changing the oil.

The bottom of the oil pan was solid black with grime and looked as if it had been used to burn trash in. I set the pan down on a rag and ran to the barn for a wire brush, some steel wool, a five-gallon bucket, and a can of gasoline.

I ran back to the tractor and put the oil pan in the bucket with the gasoline; while it soaked, I checked with Bert to see if there was anything else he needed me to do.

"No," he said, "but I want you to clean that oil pan out so good a person could eat off it."

I had my marching orders. I tackled the pan with steel wool, scrubbing it until I could make no more progress, then dipping it back in the gasoline to soak and soften. I repeated this until all the black grime was gone. Then I took a rag and wiped away all the residue left behind by the gasoline and water.

By this time Bert was ready to put the oil pan back on the tractor and add the fresh motor oil. I handed him the pan, and as I watched, he looked it over very carefully, turning it this way and that.

"Would you eat out of it?" he asked me.

"I would," I told him.

He nodded, and then told me to return the toolbox and supplies I had used to the barn. I wondered how he was going to put the oil pan back on without his tools, but I knew better than to ask. I ran the tools back to the barn and put everything in its rightful place.

By the time I returned, Bert was walking to the house, and the dinner bell had rung. I scurried to clean up and made my way to the table and behind my chair in the time allotted. And that's when I saw it.

Alton Carter

In between my fork and knife, just below the plastic cups we always drank out of, instead of my regular plate was the shiny oil pan that I had spent the afternoon cleaning.

Chapter 26
Standoff

At eleven one Saturday morning in July, in the middle of doing our morning chores, like we did every Saturday, Bert called all the ranch boys to the front yard. We could tell by the look on his face that he was upset about something. He started ranting about the importance of honesty and how someone should tell him when they broke something so he wouldn't have to find it out himself.

"You are all a bunch of thugs who couldn't function in society if your life depended on it," he said. "And you're dishonest thugs, too, which is why you are all here."

He told us he had been put on this earth to make worthless boys into young men, and we ought to be thankful that we had him as a ranch parent.

"Now stand up, put your hands behind your backs, with one hand in the other palm, facing out," he barked. "Put your heels together and point your feet in opposite directions at a forty-five degree angle."

Once we had assumed the position, he told us this was called "a military stance" and we had better get used to assuming it. He walked around and examined us one at a time, fixing our feet, straightening our backs, and adjusting our chins to what he thought was the perfect angle.

When he came to me, he got in my face: "Do you know why n------ are not allowed in the military?"

I knew better than to respond as it would only make things worse, so I just stood there looking past him. But he was on a roll that morning. He told me black people were too stupid to safely carry a gun. He said the only reason the government had welfare was to take care of all of them.

Then he addressed the group. "One of you has broken something and thrown it in the trash," he said. "That someone is dishonest, and needs to step up and take his punishment like a man."

He backed up and stood there as though one of us was going to step forward. He waited for a few seconds but no one moved.

"One of you broke the toilet paper holder in the bathroom and instead of telling me, you threw it in the trash and hoped no one would notice," he said. "Obviously whoever did this is too much of a coward to come forward, so I am going to teach you all a lesson on his behalf."

Bert told us we were going to stand there in military stance until the culprit stepped forward. Again no one moved.

"Maybe standing there in the July heat will make honest boys out of the lot of you," Bert said. And he turned and walked away, leaving us standing shoulder to shoulder, still in the military position.

Within minutes, sweat was running down our faces. We didn't dare talk for fear Bert was listening from inside the house. Nothing needed to be said anyway, we all knew no matter what he said that he intended to punish us all, even if the guilty person did step forward. So we stood there together in silence not moving an inch, waiting for him to return.

Two hours later, Bert returned with a lawn chair in one hand and a glass of water in the other. He sat down about five feet in front of us and began to drink his water.

"Just tell me who did it," he said, "and you're all free to go."

No one budged.

"Really boys, it doesn't matter who did it. One of you cowards step up and take the blame, and you can all go inside."

We knew Bert better than that, and so we continued standing in silence, looking straight ahead. He sat there a few more minutes and then took his empty glass and walked back in the house.

This time everyone started whispering to each other that it didn't matter who had broken the toilet paper holder, under no circumstances should anybody step forward. And so we kept standing.

A few more hours had passed, and we found ourselves struggling to remain vertical. The heat had become unbearable, and we were all getting dizzy and dehydrated. Some of the boys started swaying back and forth, and it looked like soon one of us was going to pass out.

After standing in line for nearly seven hours without any water, Bert returned one last time and gave us all one last chance for someone to step forward. No one moved. So this time, one by one, Bert got in our face and asked point-blank if we had done it. Again, no one said a word.

At that moment Bert knew he had lost. He stood there for a few minutes looking at us shocked and puzzled. Then out of nowhere, he told us to take our worthless selves into the house and take a shower and go to bed. We went to bed that night hungry and thirsty, but slept knowing that for once we had defeated the great Deacon Bert.

Chapter 27

I'll Be Home for Christmas

One year while still at the ranch, I decided my next Christmas was going to be different. I would be going home for the holiday, and I decided when I did, I would bring every person in my family a Christmas gift.

It would take months and months of work, but that summer I started saving my share of the hay-hauling money, and that winter I saved all the money I earned from cutting wood. I even saved most of my allowance.

Then I made a list of everybody I thought would be at my grandparents' for Christmas—eleven names in all.

We never got to go to the shopping mall or a fancy department or specialty store, but once a year Bert took all the ranch boys to the flea market north of Perkins. And I intended to do my shopping there.

The flea market was full of vendors and people selling everything from guns to homemade purses. It was all a bit overwhelming, but I shopped and shopped and shopped some more until I had bought everyone on my list a gift I thought they would like.

The Boy Who Carried Bricks

I loaded my presents up in the van and took them back to the ranch where I carefully wrapped each one, using a marker to write the recipient's name on top, so I wouldn't get them mixed-up. I stacked the gifts in my door-less closet and counted down the days until Christmas.

Christmas Eve came, and after my disastrous Christmas at the Rader facility I knew no one in my family would make the eleven-mile drive to Perkins to pick me up, so I had already planned for Bert to take me to Stillwater. I loaded my stuff in the van and made the short fifteen-minute drive to my grandparents'.

When the van pulled up in front of their house, I got out with my huge bag of gifts, feeling like a younger version of Santa Claus himself as I walked up to the front door. I could hear everyone inside laughing and talking, and I decided to go in and say hello first, so I left my presents outside by the front porch steps.

Just as I stepped inside, I heard Grandma tell everyone it was time to hand out the gifts. We didn't really exchange gifts in my family, but my grandparents always tried to make sure everyone got at least one. That was another reason I was so excited about my surprise. This year, for the first time, it would be me playing Santa Claus.

I was greeted with hugs from Aunt Faye who I hadn't seen in years. All my cousins and siblings pretty much tackled me when they saw me. And Grandma kissed me on the cheek just like she used to in better days before I helped send her son to jail.

I sat down on the floor where I used to sleep when I lived with my grandparents. And after everyone else was seated, my Aunt Faye began to pick the presents out from under the tree one by one and hand them out.

About halfway through the gift giving, I jumped up and ran outside, returning with my huge bag of gifts.

As I made my way back into the living room, Watell asked me what was in the bag. I said I had saved my money for a whole year to buy a Christmas gift for each and every one of them. I set the bag down in the middle of the floor and started handing out my gifts one at a time.

Alton Carter

My Shopping List
Grandpa—a pair of socks with a dollar bill stuck between them

Grandma—a handmade purse

Mom—a watch and perfume

Aunt Faye—a watch

Lavell—a reflector for his bike

Stevie—a wallet

Billy—a wallet

David—a lighter

Watell—some Hot Wheels cars

Kesha—a Barbie doll

Dejohn—a book with all the NFL Teams, their players, and the players' jersey numbers

After handing my presents out, I returned to where I had been sitting and noticed there was no gift in my spot. My whole family had forgotten about me, even my grandparents. I knew in my heart they had not forgotten me on purpose. I was just the grandson not living at home, so I had slipped through the cracks.

I told myself that Christmas was about giving and not receiving. And I took joy in knowing my family would never forget the Christmas that little Alton bought everyone a gift. And I told myself to remember the day that way, and not as the Christmas Alton was forgotten.

Chapter 28
The Fight Inside the Man

Bert enjoyed stirring up things, especially between Johnny and me. Johnny was about three years older, and he loved to boss the rest of us ranch kids around. To Bert, Johnny could do no wrong—and any of us who said otherwise were crybabies.

I tried to avoid Johnny, but one afternoon after he made a point of walking through the pile of dirt I had just swept up and smearing it all down the hallway floor. I had had enough.

"Idiot!" I screamed, as I got up in his face.

"Sissy!"

Name-calling turned into pushing and shoving, and before we knew it, Bert was standing at the end of the hall watching us go at each other. We both froze wondering what he would do.

"I'm sick of you two arguing," Bert said. "We're going to settle this old school. Meet me in the front yard in five minutes."

Johnny went and got his shoes. I finished sweeping the hallway and put away the trash. And then outside I went.

When I got to the front yard, Bert was standing next to Johnny with the other boys behind him.

"I'm tired of you picking fights, Alton," Bert said. "It's time for Johnny to teach you a lesson. You two are going to fight until I say stop."

Johnny and I squared off and began circling, waiting for the other to make the first move. I didn't care much for Johnny, but I really didn't want to fight him. He was older and bigger than I was. But I knew now that if Bert was involved, neither of us was leaving that yard until we fought.

Wham!

While I had been ruminating, Johnny had hit me in the face between my left ear and nose. I stumbled backwards a few steps and got hit again. Johnny's second punch landed on the right side of my head just above my eye. Now I knew I had to fight.

I ran at Johnny and hit him, swinging with my right hand and then my left landing two punches, one square on the nose and the other on his left eye. His nose began to bleed, so I backed up—hoping Bert would call the fight.

"Did you hear me say stop?" Bert said. "You'd better get at it."

Johnny swung with his right, and I leaned back causing him to miss. I faked like I was going to punch Johnny with my right, and he ducked. I drew back my leg and kicked him right in his face knocking him on his back. I ran to jump on top of him, but before I could close the distance between us he kicked me in the stomach, knocking the wind out of me.

"Get up Johnny," Bert yelled. "Get up!"

But before Johnny could, I dove on him, knocking him back to the ground. I was lucky enough to land on top, so I sat up and threw five or six punches, all of which hit Johnny in the face.

"Do you want to stop this?" I asked Johnny.

"No," he said.

Sitting on top of him, I had a clear view of the damage I'd done. Johnny's eye was swelling, his lip was busted, and his nose was gushing blood all over my shirt. He might have wanted to keep on fighting, but I sure didn't, so I climbed off him. With Johnny still on the ground, I looked up to see one very frustrated Bert.

"Keep fighting," Bert said.

"No, I'm done."

There was nothing I could have said that could have upset Bert more. He moved behind me and began kicking me in the butt. Again I told him I was done.

"I'm not going to fight anymore," I told him.

With that, Bert grabbed the back of my shirt, threw me to the ground, and then kicked me in my right shoulder. As he kicked me, all I could think about was my Uncle Stevie kicking me at the bottom of the stairs of my grandparents' house all those years ago.

Bert grabbed me by my shirt just under my chin.

"You'll do what I said, or I will personally beat the crap out of you."

When I didn't move, he told me since I couldn't be obedient I was to take a trip to the office. He let go of my shirt, and I ran down the driveway toward the front gate of the ranch.

As I ran down that dirt road, all I could think about was what I would do to Bert the next time he put his hands on me. And for the first time I considered running away. Luckily I was smart enough to realize that was exactly what Bert wanted me to do, and I was not going to give him that satisfaction.

Instead, I made it to the office and ran back to the house like he had told me to do. Bert was standing on the back porch waiting on me. I prepared myself to be hit again, but I also stepped up until I was face to face with him, and looking him straight in the eyes.

At that moment, I like to think Bert finally realized whom he was dealing with, that I was no longer scared of him. He glanced at my hands, which had become two fists clenched tight.

"I can see you still have some fight left in you," he said. "What you need is a couple of hours carrying bricks."

Without another word, I ran to the front of the ranch house and down to where the bricks were piled. Exhausted, bruised, and full of hate, I wanted to be anywhere but carrying bricks from one stack to another. The problem was I had nowhere else to go. If I ran away like I had thought about earlier, where would I go? I couldn't go home because Uncle Stevie was there. I couldn't go to my friend Tim's house because his father did not want me around. I was so alone, a boy with no one to stand up for me, no one who wanted me. I began to cry. Not because of Johnny. Not because Bert had kicked me or made me run. And for sure, not because of those dumb bricks. I cried because I was all alone and no one wanted me.

I looked up and saw Bert watching me through the living room window. He never moved or took his eyes off me until my two hours had expired.

Then he came to the front door and told me to go get a shower and get something to eat. A few minutes after finishing my shower, I was at the dinner table with a plate of food and a cup of Kool-aid. I sat at the table by myself, but I could feel Bert standing in the doorway between the kitchen and dining room. He just stood there watching me, never saying a word.

I finished my dinner and carried my plate and cup to the kitchen sink. As I walked past him, I looked up and caught him staring at me with a strange look on his face. It was like he didn't recognize me.

But one thing Bert figured out that day was that I was stronger on the inside than he thought I was. It didn't change his behavior towards me at all, but I knew he now respected me. There are a lot of bad days in my life that I would like to change, but as painful as that one was, I would live it all over again.

Chapter 29
You Think You Have Time

One weekend in 1983, I was allowed to go to Stillwater for a visit, but for whatever reason my grandparents didn't come get me, so Bert took me to them. I arrived to find my oldest brother, Lavell, sitting on the front porch. I took my bag inside and came back out, so we could talk about what we had been doing since we had last seen each other.

A few minutes later, we noticed our younger brother Watell coming down the street with a couple of his friends. As Watell got closer, we started making cracks at his expense, all the more fun because it was in front of his buddies. Picking on Watell was almost too easy. Watell had asthma and could not leave the house without his inhaler. And for some strange reason, he had a bald spot the size of a silver dollar on the top of his head.

"You need to get yourself some Rogaine, Watell," quipped Lavell.

"Sure you don't have ringworm little brother?" I chimed in. "Maybe we should take you to the vet."

Watell looked confused and started sneaking glances at his friends who were doing their best to try and not laugh. That was not acceptable to either Lavell or me. They needed to laugh. "Hey Watell," I said, "I think that bald spot on your head is an off switch. I bet if we push it, you'll fall asleep."

His friends could contain their laughter no longer. Everyone but Watell was laughing uncontrollably. One of his friends was laughing so hard he had fallen down on the ground. His other friend was running around in circles holding his side. Lavell laughed so hard he fell backwards out of his chair.

And then Watell began to cry.

He ran past us into the house, embarrassed and broken. His friends finished laughing and headed back from where they'd come from. Lavell and I high-fived each other, more than a little proud of ourselves, though deep down I think we both felt a little bad for Watell. But we just told ourselves that teasing little brothers is what big brothers do.

That whole weekend Watell barely spoke to us, and to tell you the truth, as the hours passed, we felt more and more guilty about what we had done. I knew I was headed back to the boys ranch Sunday night and it occurred to me I should probably tell Watell I was sorry. *Nah, it wasn't that bad. He'll be over it by the next time I see him,* I convinced myself.

Sunday, the van from the boys ranch came, and I left that day without saying a word to my little brother, let alone "I'm sorry."

*****

I spent Monday doing chores, cleaning the pigpens, and hauling hay from one barn to another. Tuesday we cleaned the barns and washed the ranch van. I was sitting under a tree waiting for lunch with the other guys when our ranch dad called me up to the house.

"Your grandpa is on the phone," he said.

No one from my family had ever before called me at the ranch. "Hello, Grandpa."

"Alton, Watell died yesterday."

"What did you say?" I asked.

Without any emotion, Grandpa replied, "Watell died yesterday afternoon while playing football."

My brother had suffered a severe asthma attack, according to Grandpa. And now he was gone.

I dropped the phone and fell to my knees. I couldn't cry because I was filled with anger and guilt. *Why didn't they call me yesterday? Why did they wait a whole day to call me?*

And then I remembered the last words I had exchanged with my little brother, that terrible moment in time when I made his friends laugh and caused him to cry.

*****

They buried my brother without me. And I never visited his grave for many years. After that one conversation with Grandpa, I don't recall any others about Watell. Not with my mom. Not with Grandma. Not with any of my other brothers and sisters.

It was like we just moved on without him.

And that made me wonder if my little brother had felt as invisible in our family as I did.

Chapter 30
Noticed

As far as I could tell, a lot of kids treated me just like they would anyone else. But the truth of the matter was I was anything but like everyone else. I was the only black kid at the boys ranch, living outside an all-white town.

I had a group of friends who I hung out with that accepted me despite the color of my skin, but it came at a price. Jokes about blacks and racial slurs were an everyday thing. I think everyone thought that it didn't bother me.

But it did.

The fact is no one ever asked me if the names they called black people were offensive to me. The fact that I didn't know who my father was just perpetuated the idea of African-American men abandoning their children and African-American children not knowing who their fathers are. I heard all these things so often I got used to it. I even sometimes laughed along, fearing that if I didn't, I might lose a friend. But little by little, such talk chipped away at my self-esteem.

Dating in Perkins presented another problem: I was the only black student in school. *What white girl is going to date a black guy?* I wondered. *And worse yet, if any girl did dare date me, her friends and her family would mostly likely tease or ostracize her.*

I never heard my teacher use racial slurs, but somehow I still managed to draw unwanted attention being the only black in the class. This was most common during history when we talked about slavery. It seemed that every time the word "slave" was read or mentioned in a video, everyone would turn and look at me.

Being black and playing sports in a white school also brought with it its own share of problems. My coaches often called players "nigger" if they weren't working hard. And somehow I was just not supposed to mind.

But it wasn't all bad. Since we had sheep and pigs at the boys ranch, I participated in Future Farmers of America. FFA offered me a chance to travel, show animals, and participate in speech contests. Yes, in most cases, I was the only black person at the shows and speech competitions, but I went anyway.

I was so nervous about my first speech event I stayed up all night preparing myself, but not for the speech. We were all reciting the FFA creed, and I had that down word for word. No, I was trying to prepare myself for talking for the first time before a room full of white people of all ages. All the speech competitors wore jeans, the same white shirt, and a FFA jacket, but none of that was enough to hide my hands and face.

When my name was called to give my speech, I walked up to the front of the room, settled behind the podium, and looked out over a room of everyone looking at me. I was so nervous because I wanted to be accepted. In my mind, the room had fallen silent, and everyone was staring at me because I was black.

In reality, they were staring at me because I was giving a speech. It had nothing to do with my skin color; they were just being respectful. I had never heard any racial slurs at any FFA event. I may not have made very many friends in FFA, but I was never treated as though I didn't belong.

I took second place in the FFA Creed Contest, and I was shocked. I am not sure if I deserved to be on the winner's platform or not, and to tell you the truth I didn't care. In the most unlikely of places, I had suddenly found myself feeling as if I belonged.

I attribute a lot of this to the culture of FFA, but it was also how my Ag teacher Mr. Jennings conducted himself.

About six foot tall and rarely seen without a baseball cap, Mr. Jennings was well respected in the Ag and FFA communities, which were pretty much one and the same in Oklahoma. He had a strong southern accent and always dragged out the last word of each sentence. He almost always had a dip of Skoal between his cheek and gums.

I don't know why, but Mr. Jennings always went out of his way to make me feel like I was important. He actually made the effort to come out to the boys ranch and help me pick out my pig to show. He shared with me his secret feeding recipes for pigs and sheep, and he let me ride with him to the pig shows.

I attended a lot of pig shows, and yet every time I would go to register my pig and pay my entry fee, somebody would have already paid it. I never knew for sure, but I always believed Mr. Jennings was my anonymous fairy godmother.

Chapter 31
Time to Run

Over the course of my stay at the ranch, I knew many of the boys, including myself, had repeatedly reported how we were being treated there to the ranch counselor, and finally one day Bert told us he was being fired for excessive punishment of his charges.

All we could wonder was what had taken them so long. Come to find out, a board member had stopped by the ranch the day we had been forced to stand outside for seven hours in the summer heat. Someone else had seen one of the ranch boys carrying bricks for punishment.

Watching Bert pack up and leave was one of the happiest days of my life. I remember thinking I would never have to see this man again. And I took comfort in that.

The ranch board had fired the Baitses and moved the Hamms into the house where I was living. The board had also hired new ranch parents for the other ranch house. I did not understand why the board had fired the Baitses and not the Hamms, as well. Yes, the Baitses should have been fired, but the Hamms were just as abusive. Joe Hamm shared the same punishment philosophy as Bert.

My options were limited as to how I could get myself removed from the ranch. I believed with all my heart that my caseworker would not remove me just because I did not like the Hamms. But she would be forced to place me somewhere else if I ran away. So I decided the only option I had was to run.

But running away was a lot harder than it sounded because I had no place to go. I had no idea at this point where my mom was living, and I sure didn't want to go back and live under the same roof as Uncle Stevie. *But what choice do I have?*

So the next day when Joe sent us out to feed the animals, I walked down to the barn and kept walking—into the woods behind the pigpen.

Once I was in the woods, I ran down the tree line through a pasture and crawled over the fence I had helped build. I ran down the first road I saw as fast as I could, looking over my shoulder every few seconds. I ran north along Highway 177 until I was in the middle of Perkins. Certain by now that the Hamms would have figured out I was missing and called the authorities, I got off the main street to avoid the police station in the center of town.

I was not only tired but a nervous wreck, and I still had a long way to go. I ran whenever I could, only stopping to catch my breath. By the time I made it to the gas station on the corner of Highway 177 and Highway 33, I was exhausted and realized I was in trouble.

I did my best to push through the pain I felt in my lungs. Just past the gas station, I saw a bicycle leaning on a tree in front of a house. Without a moment's hesitation, I grabbed the bike and began peddling north toward Stillwater.

Looking over my shoulder, expecting the Hamms or the police to pull up behind me any minute, I pedaled as fast as the bike would go. All was going about as well as could be expected as I traveled down the side of the highway until I noticed a black dog in a yard a block ahead. I crossed to the other side of the road hoping to avoid the dog and trying not to make any canine eye contact.

As I passed the dog, I sat up as tall as I could on my seat, trying not to look intimidated. He ran right across the highway headed my

way. I pedaled faster as the dog ran behind me, nipping at my heels. Barking and growling, the dog chased me a hundred yards or so, before growing tired and turning back for home. I had just slowed to catch my breath, when I heard another dog barking ahead of me. This dog was already on the side of the highway, waiting for me to get close enough to attack.

Again I crossed the highway to avoid the dog, but it just did the same, chasing me down the road until it too grew tired. By now I was past the point of exhaustion and needed to rest, so as soon as I was a safe distance from the second dog, I stopped on the side of the road and took a break, all the while keeping an eye on the passing cars.

A few minutes of sitting nervously on the side of the road was enough for me to gain enough strength to continue pedaling towards Stillwater. But I would do the last six miles on foot. The bicycle broke down almost as soon as I got back on the road.

I finally arrived at my grandparents' only to find no one home but Grandma. Uncle Stevie was asleep on the couch. Grandma asked me what I was doing home, and I told her that they had let me come home to visit. I knew she didn't believe me, but before she could ask me any more questions, I went downstairs and hid in one of the bedrooms.

I heard Uncle Stevie ask Grandma who had come in. Grandma told him I was home visiting for a few hours.

The next knock on Grandma's front door was Mr. Hamm and the police. Mr. Hamm told my Uncle Stevie I had run away and wanted to know if he had seen me. Uncle Stevie told him I was downstairs and they were more than welcome to come in and get me.

I didn't wait to hear anymore. I ran out the back door and jumped the fence into the neighbor's backyard. I circled the block, ran to the park, and once more took shelter in the old slide across from my grandparents' house. From that vantage point, I watched Mr. Hamm and the police talk to my grandma for a short time and then drive away.

Knowing that my relatives would hand me over to the Hamms as soon as I came home, I decided I had no choice but to turn myself in at the DHS office. When I was sure it was safe to leave the slide, I walked to DHS where I confessed to my caseworker I had run away.

"If you send me back to the boys ranch, I'll just run away again," I told her.

She agreed not to send me back but said I would have to go to the youth shelter until she could find a new place for me. She drove me to the shelter, telling them I should only have to be there for a few days while she looked for another placement. The people who ran the shelter welcomed me and went out of their way to make me feel comfortable.

The biggest shock of my stay there was when Brenda Thompson came to visit me. My old teacher told me when she had heard from my DHS caseworker that I was in town; she wanted to check in on me and see how I was doing. It was great to see her, and I appreciated her taking the time to stop by and visit. Sometimes we have more people in our corner than we realize.

Later that week, my caseworker dropped by to tell me she had found a place for me to go. There was only one option. She had not been able to find anything else for me.

*****

The day it came for me to move to my new foster home, I was a little surprised when my caseworker headed south, out of town and back to Perkins. But I did not say a word.

She pulled up to a yellow, brick house just south of downtown and parked in the driveway. As we got out of the car, I looked up at the front porch and who should be standing there but Bert and Bee Baits.

My heart sunk; I felt as if I was going to pass out. *How could this be happening to me?* I was back in the arms of the same abusive man who had just been fired for abusing boys, including me, at the ranch.

"I did my best to find you a place, Alton, but this was all I could find," said my caseworker. With my head down, and without saying a single word to Bert or Bee, I took my bags and walked into the house. Bee led me to my room, and I stayed in bed for the entire evening. I decided that very night, I was going to run away again. I just didn't know when or how.

A few days later, Bert, Bee, and I went to Stillwater to attend the same church we had attended when they were running the ranch. We sat in the pew on the very back row. While Bert was talking to someone, I asked Bee if I could go to the bathroom. I walked out of the sanctuary and headed down the hallway, right past the bathroom and out the back door of the church.

As soon as I was outside, I ran as fast as I could, stopping to duck behind cars to make sure I would not be seen.

Ultimately, I headed for my grandparents' house.

I had no intentions of staying there either, so I called my case-worker and asked her to please come get me.

Chapter 32
Boley

In 1984, I refused once again to live with my family, insisting DHS send me somewhere else.

DHS chose the youth shelter southwest of town, before sending me to a foster home in Boley, Oklahoma. I had never heard of the town of Boley before moving there. Come to find out it is one of Oklahoma's original, and still remaining, historic all black towns—one of more than fifty such towns and settlements founded between 1865 and 1920, where African-Americans were allowed to governor themselves, even in Jim Crow days.

My caseworker steered the car up a dirt drive to an old single-story white house with a small, rickety wooden porch barely being held up by wooden posts on its two corners. The house paint was peeling, and the windows looked as though they might fall out at any given moment. There was little to no grass on the half-acre the house sat on. To say I was completely in shock that my DHS caseworker had brought me to this place to stay, was putting it mildly.

"There weren't any other options," she told me. "Your only two choices are stay in Boley or go live with your grandparents."

As rundown as the place looked, I knew I had to stay in Boley. Going home was a sure way to guarantee I would drop out of school, like every other person in my family had done. And then there was the Uncle Stevie factor. Yes, Boley it was.

My soon-to-be foster parents were in their sixties and relied on the handrails to make it down the two rickety steps, coming off the porch. They introduced themselves as the Johnsons and said that they were happy to have me stay with them.

Mr. Johnson owned a shoe repair shop on the other side of town. He was a quiet man who walked with a limp because he had a prosthetic right leg from the knee down. Mrs. Johnson was a housewife and missing her two bottom front teeth. She wore a flowered dress that looked like she had made it herself.

I was sure they were good people, but based on the condition and size of their house, I was not so sure they should have been allowed to be foster parents. I hoped the inside would surprise, but no such luck. The house was really a one bedroom, and the Johnsons had converted the back porch to give it another. The result was a three-by-six room with clothes racks on two sides. In the middle of the small room, beneath the clothes, was my bed, barely visible.

The room was so small my dresser would be in the narrow hallway, outside the room. After the short tour of the house, my DHS caseworker left me in the care of the Johnsons. As I watched her back out of the driveway, part of me wanted to run after her. Instead, I joined the Johnsons in the living room where they were watching TV. Trying to make small talk, Mr. Johnson told me they had been foster parents before.

"I know our house isn't big and fancy," he said, "but it is safe for kids like you. There will always be something to eat, and you will never have to worry about being abused or neglected."

As much as I wanted an excuse to leave, Mr. Johnson's words hit a soft spot. Up until now, every place I had ever been in my life had come with someone who abused me, in some way—even at my own grandparents' and mother's. I knew then that I had to stay with the Johnsons. I had to give this elderly couple a chance.

120

We watched a television show with little conversation until I decided to turn in. As I had been taught at the ranch, before going to sleep, I unpacked my clothes and put them in the dresser outside my bedroom.

The next morning, Mrs. Johnson woke me up and told me breakfast was on the table.

"After you finish eating," she said, "we'll go enroll you in school."

*****

After breakfast, we did just that. The school was only a few blocks from the Johnsons' house, and the building housed kindergarten through twelfth grade all in the same building. The walls were made of sandstones held together with cement. And every window in the school had black metal bars on the outside.

The sidewalks leading up to the school were cracked and falling apart. The inside of the school was as bad as the outside. The walls in the hallway were dirty with paint chipping off in most places. The metal doors were rusted and barely hanging on their hinges. The metal-framed, wood-topped desks in the classrooms were covered with graffiti and carvings from past students. And the walls were devoid of educational material or decorative posters.

But what really got my attention was the students. For the first time I was in a school with all black students, teachers, and principal. And for the first time in my life, I worried that I might not act black enough.

By the time I landed in Boley, I had grown shy and soft-spoken. Years of having children make fun of the gap in my front teeth kept me from smiling or talking much. I had no idea if I would fit in at this school or not, but we were about to find out.

After getting my schedule from the office, the school counselor took Mrs. Johnson and me around and showed me where my classes were located. After the tour, Mrs. Johnson told me good-bye, saying she would pick me up after school. The counselor took me back to my first class, and the teacher introduced me as she pointed me to my desk at the back of the class. I was happy to be in the back because I did not want to be called on; I thought being in the back of the room would prevent that from happening.

*****

It did not take long for me to realize I did not fit in at school. I appreciate the irony of that, but my discomfort had as much to do with me being more of a city than a rural kid as anything else. Almost everyone at Boley spoke with a southern twang. Not only did they sound different, they all dressed differently too. I wore Wrangler jeans and loafers, with a button-down shirt, and my hair was short. Most of my fellow classmates wore oversized clothes with tennis shoes, and almost everyone had an Afro.

I was so uncomfortable, and the longer I was at the school the more I wanted to leave. I had a bad feeling that trouble was going to find me no matter what I did to avoid it.

Still the first few weeks of school passed without event; I hadn't made any friends, and I was okay with that. I just minded my own business and hoped everyone else would mind theirs. It was a plan, but one doomed to fail in a school.

Every school has its troublemakers, and one day after lunch Boley's found me. I was sitting up against the wall in the room where people gathered after lunch, when a group of boys sauntered in. They no more entered the room than everyone left—except me. I had no idea who they were or what was going on, though I did wonder where everyone else had disappeared to so fast.

One of the boys walked up to me, reached into his back pocket, pulled out a silver-and-gold knife about six inches long from the tip of the blade to the end of the handle, and pointed it at my face.

"Give me your wallet," he said.

This was trouble, and I knew it. I also knew I could take this kid if we ever fought hand to hand. But I also believed he was stupid enough to stab me if I didn't do what he said. I pulled out my brown leather wallet from the flea market in Perkins and held it out. He glanced over his shoulder to see if anyone of authority was coming then snatched the wallet from my hand.

After extracting the three dollars I had inside, he threw my wallet on the ground, then closed his knife and returned it to his back pocket. He motioned to his friends, and they were gone as quickly as they had appeared. I ran to the office and told the principal what had happened. He followed me out in the hallway where I pointed out the boy who had pulled a knife on me and taken my cash. The principal hollered for the boy, who pointedly ignored him before turning the corner at the end of the hall and disappearing.

I was expecting the principal to run after the little thief, but the principal just stood there and let the boy go. That's when I realized the principal was scared of the kid. Without saying a word, he walked back in the office, leaving me standing in the hallway.

That moment I knew I had to get out of Boley. I had to leave before I hurt someone or someone hurt me. I went back to class unable to concentrate for fear of retaliation from the boy because I had told on him. I wondered if he would be waiting for me after class. With the passing of each class period, I was expecting the worst, but I didn't see him again that day. After school let out, I made sure I stood by the office and waited for Mrs. Johnson to pick me up.

When she pulled up to the school, I walked as fast as I could while trying not to look scared and got in the car. As we drove home, I told her what happened to me at school. I told her about the boy pulling the knife on me and taking my wallet. I told her the principal hadn't done anything even after I told him about the theft and identified the boy.

"That little boy's father killed his mother," Mrs. Johnson explained to me. "His father is serving a life sentence in prison. He is living with his grandparents who are doing the best they can to control him, but they're having a difficult time with him."

As she finished speaking, we pulled into the driveway at home. I went straight to my room, set my books down on the floor, and lay down on my bed and stared at the clothes hanging on both sides of me. As nice as the Johnsons were, I knew I had to leave. The thought of going back to that school terrified me. Other than my own family and some family friends, I had spent most of my life around white kids, white teachers, and white coaches. Here I was in an all-black school, where you would think I would finally feel at home, and I felt more like an outsider than ever.

All kinds of things make people different from each other I realized, and neither blood nor skin-color was a guarantee of anything. There were good black people and good white people. There were bad black people and bad white people. I needed to learn not to judge a book by its cover. It was a cliche, but also an important lesson to learn. And I learned it in Boley.

*****

The boy who pulled a knife on me didn't show up to school for weeks following our encounter. The next I heard, Mr. Johnson said the kid had been shot and killed while trying to break into a house.

After I got that news, I immediately called my DHS caseworker, begging her to come get me. She said that it would take some time, but she would do the best she could to find me a safe place to go.

Chapter 33
Common Ground

Weeks went by without news from my caseworker. Meanwhile, I had started making a few friends at school. Among them was La-von and Ricky, two guys who, like me, believed in living under the radar and to the beat of their own drum.

Lavon was a shy kid who did well academically in school and was always willing to help me study for tests. Small for his age, he didn't seem to care when kids made fun of him. Ricky, on the other hand, was a big funny kid whose dad drove a garbage truck and who didn't let others get a chance to make fun of him, because he cracked his own jokes about being overweight.

I rounded out our trio—the shy foster kid who didn't talk or smile much because I was still trying to hide the gap in my front teeth. We were all three insecure in our own ways but in each other we found a safe haven, and friends we could trust.

By now, I was used to not having my real family around, so I no longer missed my mother and siblings. And my two new friends made life in Boley tolerable. When we weren't in school, we walked the town, dreaming of a world without bullies and sharing stories from our childhood. In the beginning, I did most of the talking, entertaining them with the series of events that had brought me to live with the Johnsons. Lavon and Ricky both knew the Johnsons and thought them nice people.

"They're definitely nice," I said, "but they sure eat some strange food."

When I mentioned the possum and turtle soup Mrs. Johnson liked to serve, both of my new friends just laughed at me.

"I'd give anything for a possum sandwich right now," Ricky said, licking his fingers.

Come to find out everyone in Boley liked possum, and according to my friends, there had to be something wrong with me if I didn't. I told Lavon and Ricky that the thought of eating the world's most ugly animal made me want to throw up.

We all got a good chuckle out of that.

*****

Ricky and Lavon were good guys, and I was glad to have them as friends. I knew they would never do anything to hurt me or get me in trouble, but they weren't enough to change my mind about Boley.

So after four months in town, I was delighted to return home after school one day to find my DHS caseworker's car parked in the driveway. She had found me a foster home in Cushing, Oklahoma.

It was welcome news, though part of me felt as if I was betraying the Johnsons, two of the nicest foster parents I would ever have. As I packed my bags, I wondered if I had made the right choice. *If Boley wasn't good enough, would Cushing be a place that I could stay? Guess I'm about to find out.*

When Mrs. Johnson told me good-bye, she made a point of saying that she saw good in me and knew I was going to make it.

"I'm sorry things didn't work out," she said, "but you are welcome back here anytime."

Disappointed in myself for having taken her hospitality and kindness for granted, I dropped my head in shame, feeling I had betrayed two people whose only crime was trying to give me a safe home and enough food. The guilt was overwhelming, as I walked out of the house and got in the car.

As we drove out of Boley en route to my new foster home, I realized the little town was not the problem: I was.

I had been abused and neglected so much for so long I was not used to people caring about me. And I didn't really know what to do if they tried, as I had shown.

If I were honest with myself, I handled abuse much better than I did someone caring about me. And I knew to have a better future, that had to change.

Chapter 34
Cushing Time

In mid-September of 1985, I arrived at my new foster home in Cushing. It was the middle of my sophomore year of high school. My new foster parents lived in a nice, well-kept, two-story brick house on the east side of town.

My foster dad, Phil, was a quiet but intimidating guy who topped six feet. Sporting a long black beard and a beer belly, he could always be found in jeans and a white T-shirt unless he was riding his Harley motorcycle, then he wore all leather. Phil owned and ran an upholstery business out of his garage called "Y-Not Upholstery."

His wife, Marcy, was a petite brunette and the more outgoing one of the two. She was a hugger and never seemed to have a problem telling anyone what was on her mind. Marcy helped in the upholstery shop at times but also managed a gas station directly across from their house.

Their home was bigger and cleaner than any foster home I had lived before and more than I could ever have wanted. My DHS caseworker told them I was a good kid who had so far managed to stay out of trouble. She also said I struggled in school, but if I tried,

I would do just fine. Phil told me he didn't care what kind of grades I made. He told me I had to go to school and that my grades would dictate how far I went in life, but it was up to me. If I wanted good grades, I would have to work hard and apply myself. If I didn't work hard in school and got bad grades, I would end up like my family.

"Either way it is up to you. I don't care," he said.

At the end of his speech, a small black dog came running into the room where we were sitting. Marcy picked up the dog, set it in her lap, and started petting it. I asked her what kind of dog it was, and she told me it was just a mutt they had rescued from the local animal shelter, and it had been with them for years.

"What's its name," my caseworker asked.

"Nig," Phil replied.

"Where did you get the name?" I asked.

Phil told me it was short for "n-----." He said they weren't prejudiced, but they had named the dog that because it was black. For some strange reason, I wasn't offended by what they called the dog. I thought it was odd, but I had spent most of my life hearing that word used by white people. I had also heard blacks call each other it, thinking it was okay so long as it was one black to another. But I knew it was a word I would never use, thanks to a conversation I once had with my grandpa about the word.

"Never under no circumstance should you ever use that word, Alton," he said. "It is wrong and unacceptable."

He told me he had grown up hearing white people call black people that, and just because blacks now said it to each other did not change the meaning. He made me promise him that I would never fight if someone called me that.

"There are things worth fighting for," he said, "but that's not one of them. People who use that word are just ignorant, pure and simple."

As I sat there with the Jones, I realized living in their home might prove to be a challenge, but I also knew if my grandpa could survive the days back when blacks were not allowed to eat inside public restaurants, when black and whites had separate water fountains, and when children of color had to go to separate schools, I could survive this. It was going to be strange hearing a dog being called that, day in and day out, but I could do it. For the time being, Nig was just a word, and I refused to let it bother me.

In spite of what the Jones called their dog, I did not believe they were racists, or surely DHS would not have allowed me to stay with them. My DHS caseworker was familiar with the Jones because she had placed other boys with them. In fact, three other foster boys were living there now; I was to meet them as soon as they got home from school.

After my caseworker left, Marcy took me upstairs to my room and helped me unpack my stuff. She said that she wanted me to feel welcome and she hoped the dog's name wouldn't make things strange. I told her that things would be fine, and I didn't care what they called their dog.

*****

By the time I got to Cushing, there was nothing I hated more than my first day at a new school. I hated thinking about meeting all the kids, wondering who would be the first one to decide to make fun of my teeth.

If that weren't enough, there were all the first day questions about who my parents were and why I was in foster care. I was tired of explaining to strangers that my mom couldn't take care of me.

So this time I decided that when I went to school, I was going to tell people that my parents had given me up for adoption, and the Jones family had adopted me. I knew the other foster boys would be home soon from school, and I anticipated the same reaction from them as I usually got from kids my age. Around four o'clock the boys walked through the door; Marcy called them into the kitchen and introduced them to me.

Chapter 35
The Boys

The first of the three foster boys I met was Allen. A senior in high school, he was a short, thin kid, with shoulder-length brown hair who dressed like a kid in a boy band. Ted was a biracial, eleventh-grader with wavy black medium-length hair who played basketball despite being only five-foot-five. Ted called himself "Magic" because he thought he played basketball like Magic Johnson. Last was James, an eighteen-year-old eleventh grader who must have thought he was James Dean reborn because he always wore blue jeans and a white T-shirt with a pack of cigarettes tucked under his right sleeve; he also wore his hair gelled, combed from front to back.

Marcy told me James would be my roommate. Besides saying their names, none of the guys really said a word, and after the introductions were over, they all went their separate ways.

That evening, we all sat down for dinner together, but once it was over, everyone once again went his or her way.

Marcy started cleaning the kitchen, and Phil went back to the shop so he could finish covering a couch that had been dropped off earlier in the day. Allen went to his room; James went to his room to finish hanging a new poster he had just bought of James Dean. All in all, the day went much better than I had expected as none of the boys made fun of me or seemed to care that I was moving in. I spent the rest of the evening watching TV and then went to bed about ten.

*****

The next morning, I got myself ready and Marcy took me to school. And sure enough, it wasn't long before a kid asked me why I had moved to Cushing. As planned, I told him the Jones had adopted me. My cover didn't last long, because the kid knew the Jones and knew I was a foster kid. I was so embarrassed; I wanted to hide in a hole. I had lied to the kid about being adopted because I was ashamed of my own family. I was also ashamed of my teeth and how I looked. Not only was I a foster kid with a mom who couldn't take care of me, but even worse I didn't know who my father was.

So far, my first day of school was a disaster, and I wasn't surprised when the school counselor found me at lunch and asked me to come talk to her. I followed her into her office, and she asked me why I had lied to my fellow student about being adopted.

"I understand being embarrassed," she said, "but that is no reason to lie. The only way the other kids are going to accept you is if they get to know the real you. Just try to be yourself, and things will work out. I promise."

I heard every word she said, but I knew she didn't understand what I was going through. She had no idea the pain that came with getting moved from foster home to foster home, even if the move was your own idea. And there was no way she could feel the guilt I carried inside my heart for leaving my own family.

Next she took me to my science class. I had no more walked in the classroom and been introduced to her, than Mrs. Powell took me back out into hall and told me she wanted to set me straight about a few things.

"I don't care if you are a foster kid or had a rough childhood. I don't feel sorry for you, and you're going to have to earn your grade in my class," she said. "You won't get any breaks from me; in fact, I'll probably be tougher on you than the other students."

Mrs. Powell had taken the time to review my school records, and she said it was obvious I was behind the other students. The more she talked, the more I hated her. *Why is she talking to me like this?* I had not been in her class two minutes, and already I was being treated like a criminal.

Mrs. Powell saw I was getting upset, and asked if I knew why she was telling me all this.

"Because you hate me because I am a foster kid," I said.

If possible, her face grew more dour.

"Most teachers are going to feel sorry for you and cut you breaks because you have had a rough life. I am not going to be one of those teachers," she said. Along with teaching science, she said she intended to teach me self-respect. That was the best she could do for me.

With a quick pat on my back, she took me back into the classroom, telling me to sit at the desk closest to hers. She grabbed a book from one of the cabinets at the back of the classroom and set it on my desk, saying I needed to spend the period reading so I could catch up. I read as she told me, until class was over. Then I waited until all the students were gone before I got up, thinking Mrs. Powell would let down her guard and be nice to me. She never even looked up. So I gathered my things and made my way to my next class.

Except for Mrs. Powell's class, every first class was always the same. I was made to stand up as the teacher read my name, introducing me to the class. I would stand up with my head slightly bowed and lift my right hand enough to acknowledge I knew my own name. I never spoke or made eye contact with anyone, and I certainly never smiled.

When school was out, Marcy was waiting in her car in the front of the school parking lot. She asked me how my first day of school had gone, and I told her about my conversation with Mrs. Powell.

Marcy smiled and said her son had also had Mrs. Powell when he was in school, and he hated her. Part of me already hated her too, but there was also something different about her. I just wasn't sure what it was. We finished our drive home and made our way into the house. Marcy asked me to go see Phil in the upholstery shop. I set my books down and went to find Phil, who was putting new fabric on a recliner. Phil had me pull up a chair to the counter where he was working and tell him how my day had gone.

"My day was fine," I said, "but Mrs. Powell hates me."

He asked me why I thought she hated me.

"I don't know," I said, "maybe because I'm a foster kid?"

Phil chuckled but kept working on the chair.

I didn't say anything about having tried to make the folks at school think Phil and Marcy had adopted me.

Finally, Phil spoke. He told me Mrs. Powell was a good teacher and I could do worse than listen to what she had to say. He said he knew his son had hated her, but I should give her a chance.

I sat out in the shop and watched Phil work on the recliner until Marcy came out and told us that dinner was ready. By the time Phil and I made it in from the shop, everyone else was sitting at the table, eating.

Chapter 36
Fistfight

As soon as I sat down, Magic asked if I wanted to hang out with him and a friend after dinner.

"Sure," I said. "What are we going to do?"

"Just hang out. Maybe walk around town," he said.

When his friends showed up, I knew I should probably have stayed home, but it felt nice to be included, even though it came at a price. Every other word that came out of the boys' mouths was a cuss word. And by the time we were out of sight of the house, all three of them started smoking cigarettes.

"You want one," one asked me.

"Nah, I don't care for them," I said.

The next thing I knew one of the boys had reached into the pocket of his baggy jeans and pulled out a joint and a lighter. He lit the joint and stuck it in my face.

"You scared of smoking weed?" he asked.

"I'm not afraid of smoking pot; I grew up watching my whole family smoke dope," I said, as I reached out to grab the joint out of his hand.

Magic snatched it before I could. He took a couple of puffs and told me that I hadn't earned the right to smoke with them. I'm not sure if Magic intervened on purpose, but I was sure glad he had. We spent the rest of the evening walking around town while the three of them smoked pot.

My next few weeks were uneventful at school, but Magic suggested I try out for the basketball team. I wanted to but was afraid if I did, I wouldn't make the cut. Magic suggested I spend some time with him playing pickup games at the park to help get me ready for tryouts. Eventually I talked myself into trying out. Ended up I wasn't the best shooter, or the most skilled dribbler, but I was the fastest guy on the court, and it was just enough to earn me a spot on the team. My name was not on the varsity list, but I had made the junior varsity team along with Magic, and we were both pretty excited about it.

When we got home, I ran into the shop and told Phil I had made the team. Phil stopped working long enough to give me a high-five. Marcy told me she knew I would make the cut.

I found basketball to be hard work but fun, and by midseason I was a starter for the JV team. Coach Neal was our JV coach, and I could tell he liked me. He was a tough coach but encouraging to all of us. I even overheard him tell the varsity coach he should give me a chance to play varsity, but the varsity coach said I wasn't good enough. Coach Neal was a short, loud, and energetic guy. Coach Farley, the varsity coach, was loud and negative. Nothing anybody did was ever good enough. We had an average season winning about half of our games, and I was sad to see the season come to an end.

*****

Meanwhile, school had become tolerable. Mrs. Powell still had me sitting by her desk, but in all of my other classes I had managed to blend into the crowd—thanks in part to my habit of sitting in the back. I had been in Cushing a few months now and had so far managed to get along without anyone making fun of me. That all changed with two bad decisions made on my way to science class. I came upon a crowd of students gathered around two boys who looked to be squaring off to fight. I pushed my way to the front of the crowd (bad decision Number 1) so I could have a front row seat to the confrontation. The crowd started yelling, "Fight, fight, fight," and that was all the excuse the boys needed to unleash their fists.

All of a sudden a boy next to me turned and said, "What did you say?" I told him that I hadn't said a word.

"I don't believe you," he said, positioning himself right in front of me, his nose two inches from mine.

"I don't want any trouble," I said. "But you need to get out of my face."

I turned to walk away, and that's when he grabbed my arm, turned me around, and hit me square on my cheekbone, below my left eye. I fell back a few steps and then (bad decision Number 2) lowered my head and tackled him. We landed on the ground with me on top of him, and I sat up and drew back my right hand to return the punch he had given me.

Just as I was ready to let fly, someone grabbed my arm and yanked me off of him. It was Mr. Lauerman, the principal, and I could tell by the stern look on his face, he was not happy. He squeezed my arm, and motioned for me and the kid I had tackled to head to his office.

The crowd quickly tried to break up, and all the kids started heading to class. But Mr. Lauerman told everyone to freeze and grabbed the two boys who had initiated the fighting, by the backs of their shirts, pulling them away from the crowd. He instructed them to go to the office as well. A tall, quiet, red-haired man who rarely smiled, Mr. Lauerman wasn't mean but he could look intimidating. He took one look at me in his office and said, "You sure didn't make it long before getting in trouble."

Before I could reply, he told me to shut up. "You'll get your chance to talk in a minute."

He called in the boy who had picked the fight with me into his office. We sat down in front of his desk, just a few feet from each other. He asked the other boy what had happened to start the fight. The kid put his head down and didn't respond.

Mr. Lauerman looked at me and asked me what happened.

"I was standing with the others watching those two boys fight when this idiot," I said, pointing to the boy sitting next to me, "asked me what I'd said. I told him that I hadn't said anything, and I tried to walk away, and then he hit me. That's what started the fight."

The principal asked the other student why he had hit me, and again the boy just sat there with his head down not saying a word. Mr. Lauerman told us we both had to sit in the office all day, for the next two days.

"What about our schoolwork?" I said.

"We'll have your teachers send it down," he said.

I didn't believe I deserved the same punishment as the other boy, but there was nothing I could do. The other two boys caught fighting were both suspended from school for a week because it was the second time they had been caught in a fight.

After school, I went to the shop and told Phil what had happened, expecting him to lecture me, but all he said was a man has a right to defend himself.

"I think you did the right thing by trying to walk away," he said.

After sitting in the front office for two days for all the world to see, I returned to classes, knowing the moment I walked into Mrs. Powell's class, I was going to get a lecture from her about how I had made a huge mistake.

Instead, all she said was that she was disappointed in me. I was not expecting that from her. I had truly thought she didn't care about me at all, but I was wrong. After class, she asked me to stay behind so she could hear about what had happened.

I told her the same story I told the principal. She seemed a bit relieved that I wasn't the one who had started the fight, but said I needed to do a better job at avoiding trouble.

"No one in the school is going to give you the benefit of the doubt, Alton," she said, "so you need to do your best to stay out of trouble."

The Boy Who Carried Bricks

Before she finished talking, Mr. Lauerman walked through the door of her class and joined in the conversation.

"I've watched you play basketball," he said, "and you're a good athlete. Playing sports might be a good way for you to stay busy and out of trouble. Have you thought of running track? The season starts in a few days."

Mr. Lauerman also told me he would like to see me play football the next year as well. Before I could agree, he gave Mrs. Powell a quick look, and then asked me if I knew she had come by the office and spoken to him on my behalf. I couldn't respond because I couldn't understand why she would have done such a thing.

I looked over at Mrs. Powell as she busily sorted papers, pretending to ignore us.

"Mrs. Powell believes in you, Alton, and you should believe in yourself."

I left Mrs. Powell's class that day ashamed of myself and afraid I had let down one of the only teachers who believed in me. I could have walked away from that kid even after he hit me. But it was too late now to think about what I should have done. Despite being ashamed of my actions the day of the fight, it felt good knowing Mrs. Powell and Mr. Lauerman wanted me to succeed. I wanted to make them proud, so I stayed out of trouble, worked hard in class, and signed up for track . . . and then football the next fall.

Chapter 37
Life Changing

The first day of football practice, I was both nervous and wondering if I would even be given a chance to play. Coach Moore, the running back coach, pulled me aside several times trying to get me to relax. And Coach Wilson, the line coach, also seemed to take an interest in me.

It became a routine after every practice for Coach Moore and Coach Wilson to make time to give me some advice as to how I could get better. They both told me that I was going to be a good player; I just needed to be patient and my time would come.

I was in my junior year of high school, and there were two senior running backs in front of me, so my chances of playing were going to be limited. I concentrated on doing what the coaches told me and trying to develop patience.

The two seniors weren't very good, but the head coach did not see the same thing in me that Coach Wilson and Coach Moore did, so I stood on the sideline during games for most of the season. Throughout the season, Coach Wilson and Coach Moore tried to get the head coach to let me in the game, but it soon became clear that as long as the two seniors were not hurt, he was not going to let me play.

My big break came when we played Guthrie. The two seniors were not doing very well, and once again Coach Wilson asked the head coach to put me in. Reluctantly, he sent me in the game with the play. It was a pass play that sent both running backs out in a pass route. My route sent me towards the sideline and then straight down the field to the end zone.

The quarterback called for the ball, and the center hiked it to him. The other running back and I ran our routes as the quarterback dropped back, looking for an open receiver. I ran for the sideline and down the field like I was supposed to do. When I reached the sideline, I looked at the quarterback and saw him drawing back his arm, planting his feet, and throwing the ball . . . in my direction. I took off as fast as I could, all the while watching the ball sail through the air downfield.

A defender beside me looked at the approaching football. The ball was on target, but the defender had the better position, and I knew he was going to intercept the football if I didn't do something fast. The ball started its descent, and the defender jumped up in the air to catch it but the ball hit his fingertips and flew back up in the air and right into my arms. I wrapped my arms around the ball, securing it against my body, and then I ran as fast as I could with the defender chasing me.

As I crossed the twenty-yard line, I looked back to find the defender only a few steps behind me, and right then he dove at my feet, clipping my right leg and causing me to stumble. He fell to the ground, and I regained my balance and ran into the end zone for the touchdown.

I couldn't believe it: my first play in a high school football game and I had scored a touchdown!

I was so happy I was smiling from ear to ear, indifferent as to who might see the gap in my teeth. I handed the ball to the referee and headed for the sideline, and that's when I saw them: Everyone on our sideline and in the stands was screaming and jumping up and down. Not just the players but also the fans. I saw Coach Wilson and Coach Moore give each other a high-five, and when I made it to the sideline, everyone on the team hit the top of my helmet or gave me a high-five or a word of greeting. The only exception was the head coach who didn't even look at me. But I wasn't about to let him steal my joy.

It wasn't the lucky catch or the touchdown that made me feel like a star that night but the sight of everyone cheering for me, for Alton Carter.

It gave me exactly what I needed to believe in myself. We ended up losing the game but for a few days at school, all people talked about was my lucky catch. Someone even hung a sign on my locker that read, "Great Catch, Alton." (I wasn't certain, but I thought the handwriting looked a little like Mrs. Powell's.)

Overnight, I had become somebody of importance to my school community, and, like any teenager pulled from obscurity to popularity, I now loved going to school. It was another important lesson. I was still the same Alton Carter I had been before the catch, but by putting myself out there, by joining the team, by practicing hard, by making that extra effort to catch that ball, I had earned people's respect. And it is amazing how much being respected has to do with being well liked.

And being liked was what mattered to me. That's all that matters to most teenagers.

The rest of the season, I never got to touch the football again in a game because the two seniors finished the season playing every offensive play. But my lucky catch stayed with me and gave me the much-needed confidence that would begin to transform me into a new and better me.

I turned in my football equipment in exchange for a basketball, and when basketball tryouts were over, I discovered I had made the varsity team. The first few games came and went, and I got good time on the JV team but I didn't get to play in the varsity games.

I knew breaking into the varsity lineup was going to be tough, but I hoped that something would happen that would allow me to prove myself to Coach Farley. And I decided to make a few changes to help that happen. I decided I would become the first one in the gym and the last one to leave. I hoped Coach Farley would notice my dedication and give me a chance.

But no matter how hard I worked, not only did he not play me, but he rarely spoke to me during practice at all. It was like he didn't even see me. One day after practice, I asked Coach Neal about it. He told me he didn't know why, but he would keep talking to the coach about how I deserved a chance to play.

I played point guard and knew I was better than the starting point guard who averaged only four points a game. I wasn't the best shooter, but I was the fastest guy on the team, and I could jump almost four inches higher than any other player and I could dunk the basketball anyway I wanted.

As the season progressed, I played better and better for the JV team. Most nights I was the team's leading scorer and played more minutes than anyone else. Christmas break was coming up, and while I hadn't been in contact with my family since I had been living in Cushing, I was missing them and wanted to go home and see them.

The only problem was we had a game during the break and missing a game got any player in trouble, even someone who would never see a minute of game time. Nonetheless, I decided to go to Stillwater and spend some time with my family.

Chapter 38
Him Again

Being back home again unleashed a flood of old emotions and memories, mostly having to do with playing with my siblings in the yard when we were children. The house hadn't changed from when I used to sleep on the living room floor with my brothers and sisters and cousins, all those years ago.

My Uncle David still lived with my grandparents while Uncle Billy was in jail for selling drugs to an undercover police officer. Uncle Stevie had finally moved out and was living in his own house a few blocks away. My two brothers and sister had moved back in with Mom who also lived just down the street.

The first day of my visit, I spent a few hours at my mom's house but never got to see my siblings. Watell, of course, was gone now, and it seemed Lavell had developed a penchant for crime while I was away. When I dropped by Mom's he had three stolen bikes sitting in his bedroom. Kesha told me she and Dejohn spent a lot of time at our grandparents' house.

While I was in the neighborhood, I even went by and visited Uncle Stevie to see how he was doing. It was a sign of how far I had come that I could do this despite the fear I felt. Uncle Stevie was also living a dangerous life, selling drugs out of his one-bedroom house.

After my rounds, I went back to my grandparents with enough time left to accompany Grandpa to an out-of-town basketball game. It was fun to watch Grandpa as a referee; he put so much passion into every hand gesture, as he telegraphed to the crowd, coaches, and players what had caused him to blow his whistle. I could tell he was as well respected as all the other referees, if not more so; the coaches on both teams always spoke to him before and after every game. He was in his element on the court or the diamond or the football field.

I still loved that man more than anyone else, and often wondered what could possibly have gone so wrong to make his children turn out like they did. Being with Grandpa that night made me realize how much I missed him—I would have given anything to spend my days with him, but I was not willing to risk putting myself back in the reach of my other family members.

On the way home, Grandpa told me he had read a story in the *Stillwater News Press* about my first touchdown. He told me he was so proud of me, and he knew I was going to be a great player.

*****

The next morning when I woke up, I called Phil and asked him to come get me.

"Is something wrong?" Phil asked. "You okay?"

"Everything is fine," I assured him. "I'm just ready to come back to Cushing."

A few hours later, Phil and Marcy picked me up and took me home. As we walked in the house, I got another Christmas surprise.

"We're getting another foster boy," Marcy said.

He would arrive later that evening, and because he had just turned eighteen, he would only be staying a few months with the Jones family since he was about to age out of the foster care system.

The news meant nothing to me. *What's one more when you already have four?* More confident in myself than ever before, I was no longer nervous or threatened by the arrival of someone new. I followed Phil into the shop. While he worked, I told him about seeing Grandpa, and how my grandpa had heard about my first touchdown and how proud he was of me.

As I was finishing telling Phil about Grandpa's comment about my potential as a football player, Marcy came in and announced the new foster boy would be there any minute. Phil stopped doing what he was doing and headed inside to wait with Marcy in the living room. I went upstairs to my room so the Joneses could meet with the new kid and his caseworker in private.

I stayed there until Phil called me downstairs to meet the new kid. Nothing could prepare me for what I found in the living room: It was Johnny, the same Johnny that Bert had made me fight at the boys ranch. I froze; I could not speak. My thin veneer of confidence had been punctured. All my insecurities came rushing in, like flashbacks from a battlefield.

Although Johnny and I never had any more fights after that first one, seeing him made me think about Bert. It was the last thing I needed just when my life was getting to some kind of normal.

What is him being here going to do to me? I couldn't say anything to Marcy and Phil—it would only make me seem selfish and jealous. I knew Phil would just tell me to let it go because it was the past. Marcy would try to make nice. I could also see Johnny was as surprised to see me as I was to see him. The moment he laid eyes on me, his body tightened and his face turned bright red. I could only imagine what my face looked like.

It took us a few seconds, but eventually we spoke, and Johnny told his caseworker he had been at the boys ranch with me a few years back. After his caseworker left, Johnny and I spent the evening catching up, sharing stories of places we had been since leaving the ranch. Johnny had returned home where he'd had several run-ins with the law. He had been placed in foster care to avoid being sent to a juvenile detention center.

The more we talked, the more the memory of our fight faded. I realized my enemy was actually a kid who in some ways was just like me. Over the next few days, we spoke on occasion but shied away from anything more. Johnny spent most of his time hanging out with his roommate, James. They both liked the same music, and they both smoked.

Chapter 39
Looking for a Reason

Basketball practice resumed with the start of school after the Christmas break, and I returned having never given a single thought about missing that one game while I was in Stillwater with my family for the holidays. I showed up for practice after school, only to have Coach Farley call me into his office and tell me to shut the door. He quickly made it clear why I was there.

"You let the team down, Alton, not showing up for the game over the break," he said. "We lost it, in part, because you weren't there to bring the ball down the court. You're the only one on the team quick enough to dribble through the full-court press, but since you weren't there to do your job, we lost."

The strange mix of compliments and criticism made me squirm, though I could tell by the look on Coach's face what he felt was more important.

"You're not a team player, Alton," he said. "You should have put the team first. Your family doesn't care about you anyway."

I wanted to ask him if I was so important to the team, why did I never get to play. But I was smart enough to know when to keep quiet. I knew Coach didn't care for me, and was possibly looking for a reason to single me out. I also knew he was right about my family. But his choice of words was wrong; they did care for me, or at least my grandparents did. I was just not a priority. For any of them.

"I'm sorry, Coach. It will never happen again," I said. "Even if you never play me, I won't miss another game. I'll be there to support my team."

I walked out of Coach's office with mixed feelings, but overall I used his words as the motivation I needed to sit on the bench during varsity games for the rest of the season if need be.

*****

Meanwhile at practice, I worked extremely hard hoping the head coach would notice my efforts. I was first to finish in all the sprints. I continued to be the first one in the gym and the last one to leave.

But game after game, Coach would walk up and down the bench grabbing different kids and putting them in the game. I did my best to catch his eye as he walked back and forth, hoping eye contact would force him to play me. It didn't. But I was still playing JV, and in most games I was the second leading scorer and leading rebounder. Coach Neal played everybody in the JV games.

"The only way you get better," he said, "is by gaining experience on the court."

Player development is also the point of having a junior varsity squad, and thanks to Coach Neal not only did I gain experience but confidence as well. I was doing what smart, underappreciated, ambitious players have done since the beginning of time: I was preparing myself for my moment of opportunity. I just never thought it would come in the form of a twisted ankle.

But who was I to question fate. And sure enough with the season almost over, one of the starters turned his ankle during practice, and his doctor advised him not to play in the few remaining games of the season. As sorry as I felt for the guy, I knew this might be the chance I had been waiting for . . .

And sure enough the very next game, Coach put me in. True, the team we were playing wasn't very good and we had a twenty-five-point lead, but it still felt good when Coach Farley called my name.

"Carter, get in the game." I jumped up from the bench and ran down the sideline past the rest of our players and coaches. At the scorer's table, I waited until the ref motioned me into the game. It was our ball and my job to inbound it.

I was so nervous I made a beginner's mistake. Instead of passing the ball to one of our players, I stepped over the line and dribbled the ball down the court. The ref blew the whistle, and I froze while he took the ball out of my hands. The whole gym was looking at me in shock and rightly so. This was a varsity game. Varsity players didn't make mistakes like the one I had just made. Suddenly I wished Coach had never relented and put me in the game.

Embarrassed and nervous, I looked over at our bench. Coach Farley was staring at me in disbelief.

"What the heck are you doing, Alton?" he hollered.

I had no good answer so, wisely, I said nothing. One of my teammates came to my rescue, telling me it was okay and not to be nervous. Another player told me to shake it off and concentrate on playing defense.

Sometimes the best thing to do is the simplest thing. So I did what they told me and survived the rest of the game without making another mistake.

After the game, several people came up and told me I had played a good game. I knew I hadn't played well, but it sure made me feel better hearing people say otherwise.

In fact, with each of their encouraging words, my confidence grew until I came to believe in my ability to play basketball. I didn't score more than a few points in the last two games of the season, but I had become important enough to get playing time. And that was a victory in and of itself.

After the last game, we handed in our gear and cleaned out our lockers. I hated to see the season come to an end, but was glad it had lasted long enough for me to become a contributor to the team.

The Boy Who Carried Bricks

We also learned Coach Farley was moving to a different town so we would be getting a new coach next year. I wondered if Coach Neal might be promoted to head varsity coach, but I kept my speculation to myself, and my thoughts turned to spring sports.

Track practice had already begun, so my after-school activities moved from inside a gym to an outdoor track. Our track team wasn't very good, and in hindsight I realize we didn't really work or run enough to deserve to be any better. But the coach cared a lot about kids.

Like the previous year, I ran the 400-meter relay, the 800-meter relay, the mile relay, and the 400-meter. Our track team was a close group, and Coach Moore didn't seem to mind that we under trained and underperformed. At most meets, the highest our runners placed was third.

When Regionals came around and Cushing didn't qualify for state, it was really no surprise. Track season was over, and I was excited to take a break from sports. Only a few weeks remained of school, and I wanted to spend my free time doing nothing or sitting in the shop with Phil.

Chapter 40
Metamorphic

School was almost out, when my DHS worker called, saying she had made an appointment with an orthodontist to see about me getting braces. My appointment was for the next day. Her call triggered a wave of emotion. All I could think about was how my whole life I had done everything I could possibly do to tame my laugh and rein in my smile so no one would notice my teeth.

Braces were a gift so good, and so expensive, I had never dared to even wish for them. I had just assumed I would spend the rest of my life hiding my teeth.

I hung up the phone and ran upstairs to the bathroom, where I stood for what seemed like hours looking at my teeth in the mirror and dreaming of what they were going to look like once the gap was closed. *I'll be able to laugh out loud like everyone else*, I thought.

I walked out of that bathroom taller than when I went in and went to bed that night excited for my transformation to begin. The night seemed to last forever, and I didn't sleep a wink.

The next day my caseworker and I drove to Stillwater to a brown brick building with a sign on the front door that read "Dr. Stewart's

Orthodontics." The waiting room was full of patients, and for every patient that left the office, another one came in.

When it was my turn to be seen, Dr. Stewart made a point of saying that he was glad to see me. "I'm going to give you a smile you can be proud of, Alton," he said.

After a brief exam and a quick conversation with my caseworker out front, Dr. Stewart returned and told me he was going to put my braces on that very day. And so he did.

On the way back to Cushing, my teeth began to hurt but the doctor had told me to expect that as the braces did their work. My caseworker told me that she was happy for me, but she didn't want me to be hurt if kids teased me or called me names like "brace face" or "railroad tracks." It was kind of her to worry about me, but I quickly set her straight.

"I don't care what they call me," I told her. "Whatever name they can come up with is better than what I have been called up to now."

I meant what I said, but I was anxious to see how my friends at school would react when they saw me. The next morning at school went as I expected: Everyone noticed. And everyone gave me a hard time. And, yes, kids called me new names and teased me about getting braces at my ripe old age.

And it was worth it all.

For the first time in my life, getting teased about my teeth made me feel good. And within a few days the teasing stopped—that tends to happen when you're comfortable in your own skin. More and more my life seemed like the life of one of those happy, normal, ordinary kids whose lives I had always envied.

But even I never dreamed "ordinary" would feel so good.

The school year was over, and it was time for Johnny to leave the Joneses', but before he could be officially moved he told me he was going to run away. He was afraid the courts were going to send him to jail; running away seemed like his only option.

I didn't really believe him when he told me, but sure enough the next morning Johnny was gone. I worried he had ruined his chances for a better life by leaving, but part of me was glad he was gone. Looking at him had always brought back our time at the boys ranch, and I was doing my best to erase the memories of that place.

I had never told Johnny, though he might have been the one person who would have understood, but I had found letting go of some of the terrible things that happened in Perkins was much harder than I was willing to admit.

Chapter 41
First Love

That summer, because I still didn't have a car, I rode the bus from Cushing to Stillwater everyday to my summer camp job, along with the local campers from my town. Those bus rides were some of the best of times I had with the campers. We sang songs and played games the entire thirty-minute ride to and from the OSU campus.

A few weeks into camp, I noticed a new girl, Jamie, working with the fourteen-year-olds. She had long, curly black hair, and I thought she was cute. I spent the next few weeks finding reasons to see her but never had the nerve to speak to her. If she ever had reason to look at me, I made sure our eyes never made contact. I preferred staring at her from a distance, admiring everything she did.

That all changed but not because of anything I did. One day, Jamie just walked up and sat down beside me at lunch. She glanced at me several times, but I sat there frozen not knowing what to do. A few minutes passed in uncomfortable silence.

"Why have you been watching me?" she asked.

Suddenly I couldn't swallow the food in my mouth. I tried to take a drink, but my hands were shaking so much I spilled my drink down the front of my shirt. Jamie just laughed. "Never mind, Alton. I know you've been watching me," she said. "But if you like me, you should at least talk to me."

I wasn't sure what a heart attack feels like, but I'd have sworn I was having one. I managed to calm down enough to introduce myself, apologize, and promise I would not stare at her anymore.

"I don't care if you stare at me. I just think if you're going to, you should at least talk to me, too."

With that she grabbed her tray and left me sitting at the table, with my ten-year-old campers singing, "Two Little Love Birds Sitting in a Tree." I told my charges to stop, but it just seemed to make them sing louder. Deep down I hoped the first part of the song would come true.

My promise not to stare already forgotten, I searched the room for Jamie to see if she was paying attention to the song my group was singing. I spotted her on the other side of the lunchroom, and I am certain she heard the singing because as soon as our eyes met, she blew me a kiss. My heart melted into my stomach.

She had instantly transformed in my eyes from cute to beautiful, and I wanted her to be my girlfriend. But I had never had a girlfriend before, and I wasn't sure how to make that happen. As I gathered up my campers and headed to our next activity, all I could think about was Jamie and how I was going to ask her to be my girlfriend.

I decided I would write her a note. It was a pretty juvenile overture for a high school upperclassman but then I was new at matters of the heart. I wrote, "Dear Jamie, would you like to go out with me? Circle yes or no and give this back to me tomorrow."

When it was time to board the buses for home, I waited until Jamie was boarding hers to run up and hand her the neatly folded note. I ran to my bus without looking back, hoping she would wait until she got home before she read it. Her bus was barely out of sight, when I started second-guessing myself about giving it to her.

Regret was also setting in. I spent the rest of the day playing out various scenarios of what would happen when I saw her the next day. I was nervous one minute and sick to my stomach the next. But if I was honest with myself, I think I was more nervous about the idea of her actually going out with me than her telling me she just wanted to be friends.

The next day at camp I did my best to hide from her. I wanted to delay what I now considered to be my inevitable brush off as long as I could. A tap on my shoulder jerked me out of my thoughts. I turned to see Jamie standing there with my note in her hand. I reached out and took the note, and she smiled at me, like only she could, and walked away.

With my hands shaking, I unfolded the paper and went right to the bottom to see her answer. But neither the yes, nor the no was circled. Instead, at the bottom of the note, she had written, "If you would like me to go out with you, ask me in person."

I folded the note up and stuck it in my pocket. I looked for Jamie, and found her standing on the other side of the room, looking back at me. I waved to her and then escorted my group to its first activity.

*****

Throughout the day my campers tried to talk to me, but they might as well have been speaking Greek. I was too consumed with what I was going to say to Jamie.

By the end of the day, I was no better off than I had started.

As the campers started getting on the buses, I went into full panic mode. That's when Jamie walked right up to me and asked if I was going to ask her out. It was a miracle, right? All I had to say was, yes. Instead I froze again, with my heart beating so fast I wanted to pass out. But I was no fool. Inexperienced, yes. Stupid, no. Before she could walk away, I swallowed the lump in my throat and spoke.

"Would you be my girlfriend?" It wasn't exactly asking her out as requested, but it was what I wanted. And the question seemed to please her.

"Yes," she said, with a smile. And then she kissed the tip of her fingers on her right hand and placed them on my cheek. As she turned to head to her bus, I was left standing with what I am sure was a silly look on my face and only one thought: *I can't believe I have a girlfriend!*

The rest of the summer went by so fast. We talked and spent as much time together at camp as possible, but it never seemed enough. She lived in Stillwater and I lived in Cushing so seeing her outside of camp was not an option, or it wasn't until I figured out if I visited my family in Stillwater, I could go see her as well.

After making arrangements with my grandparents, I called Jamie and told her I would be in Stillwater for the weekend, and would she like to do something together. She agreed, saying her mother wanted to meet me.

Chapter 42
The Lie

When I arrived in Stillwater, I got my uncle to take me over to Jamie's. A woman in military fatigues answered my knock. She told me to come in and have a seat on the couch next to Jamie.

"Why should you be allowed to date my daughter?" she asked bluntly.

I had no idea how to answer that question, so I kept it simple.

"I like her," I said.

It was obvious she did not like my answer, and I wasn't sure what else to say. She proceeded to tell me that she was a ranking officer in the military and she had high expectations for her daughter. She was not going to let her daughter date just anyone.

"I have worked very hard as a single parent to provide for my family and to raise my daughter," she said, "and I'm not going to let some boy ruin her."

For someone with as little dating experience as me, it was a tough first date. The only thing missing was a dad with a shotgun, and I couldn't help thinking that as a member of the military, that could be her next move.

"Tell me about yourself," Jamie's mom said.

I told her I lived in Cushing, was involved in sports, and wanted to go to college. I told her my parents owned an upholstery store and managed a gas station. She seemed to approve but ended our conversation with two warnings: "You'd better always treat my daughter with respect . . . and you'd better keep your hands off her."

Her speech finished, she got up and went into the kitchen. Jamie and I talked for a while, until it seemed time for me to leave. Jamie followed me on to the front porch. I hugged her and walked away, already racked with guilt because I had lied to Jamie and her mother. *What was I thinking calling Phil and Marcy my parents? Don't you remember the last time you lied about that? It did not end well.*

I hadn't done it on purpose. Instinctively, I just knew Jamie's mom would have a problem with me being a foster kid. I also realized I had never told Jamie I was living in a foster home because my family home was not the best place for me. It was not a secret I could expect to keep very long, even in Stillwater.

I spent a lot of my summer in Stillwater with Jamie, but it came at a price because the only place I had to stay in town was with my grandparents. Life at their house hadn't changed. The house was still dirty; people still drank and fought and smoked dope; and Grandpa still did everything he could to get away from it all. I loved my family very much but I wanted nothing to do with them.

Being a foster kid was better but it wasn't ideal. Sometimes it had been scary and horrible. But it had also helped me realize that a lot of what went on at my grandparents' was not normal, or healthy. Some of my foster homes hadn't been perfect, but any one of them was better than anything my family had provided. I knew it was just a matter of time before Jamie and her mom found out my secret, but they were not going to hear it from me.

*****

A few days before school started, Jamie told me her mom had gotten new orders. They would be moving to London by the middle of the school year. I couldn't believe what I was hearing. Every inch of my being wanted what Jamie said to be a bad joke. I realized it wasn't when Jamie began to cry.

We spent that evening sitting on her porch, holding hands, and wondering if there was anything two teens could do to alter the future.

Knowing she was leaving soon, it seemed the time to tell her I was a foster kid living in Cushing. Jamie quietly listened as I told her what had led me to leave my family. I finished and waited for the rejection I felt sure was to come.

"I already knew about your situation, Alton. Lavell told me a while ago. I ran into him at the park, and he told me you were living with a white family in Cushing. I asked him what was he talking about, and he said you'd left your family because you thought you were too good for them."

And then she told me her mom knew my mom, and she had been worried someday their paths would cross and they would put two and two together.

"I'm so sorry I lied to you, Jamie," I said. "Should we go tell your mom the truth?"

"Let's just enjoy tonight," she said, "and we will worry about telling Mom later."

Chapter 43
Down Goes Stevie

That night when I returned to my grandparents' I found my Uncle Stevie sitting on the front steps, drinking whiskey. I told you not much had changed around at Grandma's. I lowered my head to avoid eye contact and headed for the front door—praying my uncle would leave me alone.

But as I passed him on the stairs, he reached up, grabbed my arm, and jerked me to a stop.

"You forgotten what you did to me?" he asked.

I knew what he was referring to but played dumb.

"Don't know what you mean," I said quietly.

He gave me a hard look. "You got me thrown in jail," he said.

The familiar smell of alcohol on his breath brought back memories of that night, of him throwing me down the stairs, of him kicking me until I thought I might die, of me running from the house, nowhere to go.

He squeezed my arm hard, and tears of hate began to run down my face. I jerked my arm out of his grasp. He tried to come after me, but he was so drunk his wobbly legs betrayed him, and he tumbled down the stairs. He landed on the ground with whiskey all over his shirt. He let out a gurgling moan; I ran inside and shut the door. Inside I dialed Phil's number and asked if he would please come get me.

"I'll be there as soon as I can," he said.

I hung up the phone and went to tell my grandparents Uncle Stevie had fallen down the stairs. Grandma jumped up out of her chair and ran outside to check on her baby. Grandpa continued watching TV as if nothing had happened. I went upstairs and packed my bags.

When I finished, I went downstairs and peeked out the front door just as Uncle Stevie was telling Grandma I had pushed him down the stairs. As soon as I heard that, I grabbed my bag and ran down the stairs and out the backdoor and hid. I could hear Grandma, still in the front yard, screaming for me to get out of her house and never come back.

It took thirty minutes for Phil to arrive. As soon as I saw his car, I ran out and climbed in telling him we needed to leave right this minute. As we drove away, Grandma appeared in the front door— shaking her fist in the air and screaming curses at me.

As we drove out of Stillwater, I told Phil in detail what had happened with my Uncle Stevie this night and all those other nights so long ago. When I finished, all he could say was he didn't understand why my grandma would treat me that way.

We rode the rest of the way home in silence.

When we got home, I thanked Phil for coming and getting me, grabbed my bag, and ran up to my room. In the dark, I pondered what I could have done to make my grandmother hate me so much. She knew her son was an alcoholic and wife-beater. After all, she was the one who picked his whiskey bottles up off the floor. And she had seen him beat the women in his life.

And yet, when forced to choose between her abusive son and a defenseless grandson, she stood by her son. *Maybe she thinks of me as a traitor because I left them*, I thought.

I knew I felt guilty about leaving my siblings behind. But I also knew when it came to taking abuse I was the weakest of all the grandkids, and if I had stayed, I would not have been able to protect them or me from Uncle Stevie or the men Mom brought home.

I thought about how I always cried longer than my siblings after the beatings. They had survived by growing hard; I had left because denying my feelings and denying my conscious was not an option for me.

As I looked back on all that had brought me to this moment in my life, I realized that if I had the choice to leave home all over again, I would do the same thing.

I knew in my heart I had come too far to turn back now, so I told myself that while saving myself was a selfish act, ultimately in being selfish, I was giving myself a fighting chance to become a respected, productive member of society. And didn't I owe myself that?

Chapter 44
Good-bye

With a few weeks of summer break left and football practices starting soon, I made arrangements to go visit Jamie for the last time of the summer. As usual, I had Phil drop me off at my grandparents' house, but this time I did not step foot in the place.

I walked up on the front porch and waited for Phil to drive out of sight so I could run across town to visit Jamie. It wasn't that I was hiding my visits with Jamie from Phil, but more that I didn't want him to know that I was avoiding my family. And I sure didn't want my family to know that I was in town and wasn't coming to visit.

As I ran across town to Jamie, something inside me felt different. But I couldn't put my finger on it.

The look on Jamie's face when I saw her told me all I needed to know: they were leaving for London as soon as possible.

A pain I had never felt before started in my chest. The only girl I had ever loved was leaving me. I had been beaten and abused in the past, but now I knew the pain of a broken heart.

It was time to say good-bye.

"Good-bye, Jamie," I said. "I will never forget you."

Jamie hugged me tighter than she had ever hugged me before, gave me a kiss, and walked back in the house without ever saying the two saddest words in the dictionary.

I watched the door close and I knew in my heart it was the last time I would see her. And I was right.

When I later tried several times to get Jamie's new address in London from her grandmother, she wouldn't give it to me. Finally, she told me why.

"You're not allowed to contact her," she said, "you aren't who you said you were."

Chapter 45
Football

Days later, football practice started. I hoped it would take my mind off of losing Jamie, but broken hearts aren't so easily managed. And at times I really struggled.

Practices were extremely competitive because five guys were vying for the position of running back, and I knew I had to focus and bring my A game if I wanted to be the starter.

With Coach Moore now the head coach, I had a good chance if I could prove myself the top candidate. Sure enough, when the starting varsity lineup was announced, I was named the starting running back and given the jersey number 41.

Being a starter stoked my confidence. My first game I scored three touchdowns and ran for more than a hundred and fifty yards. I led most 3A schools in touchdowns and average yards per carry. My name appeared in the sports page almost every week, and by the end of the season, I was on top of the world.

One of the highlights of my senior year football season was the night my grandpa showed up to referee one of our home games. I had no idea that he was coming but was excited he was there. I thought he might come and wish me good luck before we took the field, but kickoff came and went, and my grandpa never said a word to me.

My game got off to a slow start. By halftime, I had fumbled the ball twice. Inside the locker room, Coach Moore pulled me aside and told me I needed to stop trying to impress my grandpa and just play football.

"I can tell you're nervous. It's normal," Coach said. "You just need to relax and have fun."

I told Coach I was upset because my grandpa was one of the referees, and he wouldn't even speak to me. Coach said he knew my grandpa was out there, and so did everyone else.

"Your grandpa isn't speaking to you because he is a professional. He doesn't want to give anybody a reason to think he is playing favorites. That's something to be admired, not something to whine about."

I knew Coach was right. When the second half started, I was ready to play.

I ran for a fifty-yard touchdown in the third quarter, and while my grandpa couldn't give me a thumbs-up or a pat on the back, it was enough to know he had been there to see me run into the end zone.

In the fourth quarter, at third and fifteen, Coach called one of my favorite plays, the twenty-eight pitch.

We lined up in formation, and the quarterback got under the center and called for the ball. "Down, set, hut, and hut."

He turned and pitched me the ball, and I turned right towards the stands. I turned up field and ran along the sideline past the first down, headed for the end zone.

About forty yards out, in my peripheral vision, I saw someone running beside me to my right, near the sideline. Afraid I was about to be tackled, I gripped the ball tighter and did everything I could to gain enough speed to make it past the goal line.

At the twenty-yard line, I turned and looked for the defender, and that's when I saw him. It wasn't a player running beside me. It was my grandpa. He ran beside me past the goal line, stopped in the end zone, blew his whistle, and stuck both arms straight up in the air, signaling a touchdown.

As my teammates gave me high-fives and slapped me on top of my helmet, I looked over at grandpa and he gave me a wink. It will always be one of the best moments of my life.

We lost the game that night, but when I came out of the locker room, Grandpa was standing near the door waiting to talk to me.

"It was a proud moment, running down that field with you," he said. "I'll never forget it."

I wanted to reach up and give him a hug, but he was not the hugging type, so instead I shook his hand and walked him to his pickup. As my grandpa crawled in his truck, I told him I loved him.

"I'm so glad you got to see me play," I said.

"I'm glad as well, son."

And then he was gone.

*****

The very next Friday was Senior Night, and I was in a dilemma. I wanted my grandparents to walk out on the field with me, but I also thought Phil and Marcy should be out there. If anyone had had a part in my Cushing turnaround, it was those two.

I decided to ask Phil, Marcy, and my grandparents. Phil and Marcy were excited about being asked and told me they wouldn't miss it for the world. My grandparents also promised to be there and said they were looking forward to it.

"I'll call you later and remind you," I said when I called them, "so you don't forget the date."

The big day came, and four minutes before kickoff my grandparents had yet to arrive. All the seniors and their parents were lined up on the Cushing sideline near the end zone, waiting for the ceremony to begin. I paced back and forth hoping my grandparents would make it before the ceremony started. One at a time, the announcer started calling the seniors out to the midfield to introduce them along with their families. There were four seniors in front of me, so I still had hopes Grandma and Grandpa would somehow walk out on the field right as they called my name. "Alton Carter, Number 41," the announcer called.

Still no Grandma or Grandpa. Phil and Marcy proudly escorted me to the fifty-yard line, where they were introduced as my parents. I did my best to hide my disappointment, but I couldn't fool Marcy.

"I'm sorry they didn't make it, Alton," she said.

The ceremony over, parents began to make their way into the stands, and I joined the other players in the end zone for warm-up.

And that's when I saw my grandpa's truck pull into the parking lot. I was disappointed and hurt, but not just for myself; I was embarrassed for them as well.

By the time they made it into the stadium, they realized they had missed the ceremony. I felt awful for them. They had both dressed up for the occasion. Grandpa had on a silver suit with a white shirt and black shoes. Grandma wore a purple flower print dress and a silver hat and purse that matched grandpa's suit. Once they realized they had missed the ceremony, they went and sat up in the stands until halftime, when they left without saying good-bye.

Chapter 46
Good Times

Football season came to an end, and it was time for basketball with yet another new coach. Our season was uneventful, and we ended up winning more games than anyone predicted. Even though at best we were an average team, we all got along well and enjoyed basketball more than ever before. Coach Fixico didn't require us to practice as much as our old coach, so it gave us more time to spend together. And that's how I came to be friends with Lance Hoggat.

During basketball season, Lance started inviting me over to his house to eat, and before long I was spending the occasional night there, too. On game days, Mrs. Hoggat would prepare snacks for the two of us, decorating paper sacks and filling them with drinks, candy, and her famous cookies. Lance and I loved her cookies because she wrote our jersey numbers on the top of them in icing. On days that we had away games, she would bring the gift bags up to the school and leave them in our lockers.

All in all it was a good basketball season, and I was thrilled when my grandparents made it, on time, to Senior Night. Phil, Marcy, and my grandparents walked with me to center court on that special night. My grandparents even came over to Phil and Marcy's after the game and spent a few hours visiting.

It was hard to recognize my grandmother as the same woman who had once screamed at me to never darken her door again. On this night, she seemed like she had never been more proud of anyone in her life as she held my senior plaque in her arms and told me how proud she was that I was her grandson. It meant a lot to hear her say that, and my senior year of high school was that much better for it.

*****

Track season kicked off with yet another new coach—a loaner from the girls basketball team. Earl Madison was a tough, passionate coach who loved working with student athletes. He was just as demanding on the track field as he was on the basketball court, and he gave us no option but to give our absolute best.

Every day he had elaborate workouts for every person on the team. We started each practice with stretches and moved to running drills. After a week of practice, he assigned us our events. He put me on the 400-meter dash, 400-meter relay, and the mile relay. I absolutely hated the 400-meter dash and begged him to give it to someone else, but he told me it was mine to run all season.

I struggled to place higher than fifth or sixth place in the dash, but Coach Madison made it clear he knew my only problem with the event was my attitude, and he was not about to let me give up on it no matter how much I hated it or dragged my feet. He told me he had watched me play sports the last two years, and he knew I was a great athlete.

More importantly, he knew I did not easily give up.

"I watched others play before you, when everyone knew that you should have been given a chance," he said. "But you sat on the bench with a good attitude anyway, when others would have quit. Bring that same positive attitude to the 400-meter dash, and you'll soon be fairly good at it." His words made sense. And it meant something to know he had noticed me during those early years at Cushing High.

So I took his advice and spent the next few weeks working to improve my 400-meter time. Darn, if the man wasn't right.

By Regionals, I had improved enough to qualify for State.

I knew my chances of winning or even placing at State were slim to none, but I lined up on the track in Lane 5 that day, ready to do my best for my team, my school, and my coach. The gun sounded, and I came out of my starting position and headed around the first curve, lengthening my stride down the back straight away. Little by little, I began gaining on the three runners in front of me. We began rounding the second curve, and I noticed the runner in Lane 4 was gaining on me with each step he took. Watching him pass me was hard; I wanted to sprint to keep up with him. But I was determined to run like Coach had trained me and save my big push for the final straight away. I still had some energy left, but by the time I entered the final straight away, runners in three lanes had passed me and the runner in Lane 5 was ahead of me and starting to increase his lead.

That's when I heard Coach yell, "Now Alton!"

I dug deep inside of me and ran as hard as I could with everything I had. The runner in Lane 5 and I exchanged leads several times, but just before I crossed the finish line, I leaned forward and beat him by a nose, earning a fourth place finish in the State track meet. Coach was so proud he ran out on the track, hugged me, and told me what a great race I had just run.

Coach was the kind of person you didn't want to disappoint. He had a way with words and always encouraged and inspired us to give our best effort no matter how great the odds. His heart was as big as the track we ran on, and we were all better for having known him.

*****

It was our last week of school, and we were all excited about graduation. Most of my classmates planned on skipping some or all of the week, but I decided I was going to go and enjoy as many days at Cushing High as possible. I would not have missed the last few days of school for anybody or anything. I felt like I owed it to my teachers, coaches, and my foster parents to complete what I had started. When I finally walked across that stage in May of 1988, I was so proud I could hardly keep from crying.

I was not class valedictorian nor did my name appear on the honor roll, but I graduated with honor, the honor of being the first person in the history of my family to ever graduate from high school.

Although the only people to show up for graduation were Phil and Marcy, they were enough. I had decided beforehand if my biological family didn't make it, I would not let their absence steal my joy or my pride in what I had accomplished.

I had done something my relatives had let slip away. I knew I was the lucky one.

And to top it all off, I signed a letter of intent to play football for Southwestern in Winfield, Kansas.

Epilogue
Full Circle

I would go on to graduate from college but from Oklahoma State University, not Southwestern. There were a few bumps along the way, but earning a bachelor's degree would be another first for my family.

In 1990, I met the woman who would become my wife. It was love at first sight. I introduced myself to Kristin with one question: "Will you marry me and have ten kids?"

We did marry, though so far we only have two sons, but I am still a pretty young guy.

I was honored to become a police officer, but eventually Kristin encouraged me to follow my passion and find a way to work with children. I became involved in the local Stillwater community, helping develop youth anti-drug programs while also volunteering at the Stillwater Community Center.

Eventually, I gained enough confidence to share my own story with others, and soon I was traveling all over Oklahoma as a motivational speaker, sharing the highs and lows of my life in hopes of helping someone else.

There have been good years and bad. Successes and failures, but eventually I ended up where I was meant to be. In February 2007, I was hired to be director of youth ministries at the First United Methodist Church in Stillwater, Oklahoma. Seven years later, I'm still there, still working with young people.

One of my favorite outreach programs at the church is the free community dinner we serve every Thursday evening. It isn't unusual for a hundred and fifty people to join us for it. Our church hosts it, but lots of clubs and individuals and other churches volunteer their time to make the meal possible.

One Thursday I dropped by to help. The parking lot was already full of cars, and I could see a long line of people waiting patiently to get their plate of food. I made my way inside and before I could be put to work, I heard someone call my name.

"Alton! Alton!"

The voice sounded familiar and when I turned around I knew why. It was my middle-school principal, Mr. Mills, who I had not seen since sixth grade.

We spent the next thirty minutes catching up. Mr. Mills told me he had retired but kept himself busy by volunteering.

"What are you doing here?" he asked.

"I'm the youth minister here," I said. "And when I'm not working or volunteering, I'm writing a book about my life."

Mr. Mills eyes lit up, and he asked me if I would be interested in coming and giving a talk to his Lions Club. The Lions have always been big supporters of the boys ranch in Perkins, and so I told him I would love to come speak but he needed to know I didn't have many positive things to say about my stay at the ranch.

"But I did learn the value of hard work in my time there," I said.

Mr. Mills said he had not been aware of any trouble at the ranch with the treatment of the boys but agreed it might be best to keep that part out of my talk.

"It might rub some of the members the wrong way," he said. "The ranch is making a positive impact on kids today. Do you know Bryan Larison, the ranch executive director?"

The Boy Who Carried Bricks

I nodded. "I've spoken with him in the course of writing my book, and he gave me permission to tell the truth about the ranch as it was at that time. I've also visited the ranch and have done a few activities with the boys. They've made lots of improvements to the facilities and how they treat the boys."

We finished our conversation with a promise that we would do the talk as soon as possible, and when I spoke I would tell the whole story about my time at the ranch, good and bad. And sure enough, a few days later I was standing behind a podium telling my story to a room full of Lions Club members.

I was still a little nervous about how they would receive my sad tales so I told a few positive stories first. Several times I found myself clearing my throat and doing my best to look past the crowd as I described how we were punished there. Only a few people in the audience had been members then, and I couldn't help wondering how they felt hearing about the oil pan incident and the use of the bear crawl and the racial slurs I had endured.

By the time I finished describing my life at the boys ranch, the room was quiet. And for a brief moment it felt like I was at a funeral. I ended my talk by explaining how I had come to write a book about my experience and that writing a book had been a dream of mine since high school.

My motivation for writing *The Boy Who Carried Bricks* was to tell my story in hopes it would make a difference in some reader's life. I wanted it to inspire teachers to strive to be the best they possibly could be and to know that they have an opportunity to give kids a chance to believe in themselves—even the seemingly most hopeless of children.

I wanted DHS personnel to read it and understand the importance of their role as protectors of our youngest citizens, the importance of continually striving to improve our social and foster care programs—and the importance of finding safe places for children and always being on alert for a child in trouble or danger.

I wanted children who are being or have been abused to read it and know they can become whatever they dare to dream. I wanted young people blessed with good families and all they need to appreciate what they have and be willing to share with those less fortunate.

I told the group I wanted anyone who read my book to find something in it that would inspire them to do whatever they could to make this world a better place. I thanked them for listening and for making a difference in the lives of children.

"The boys ranch wasn't perfect in my day," I said, "but it was still far better than living with my real family."

I stepped away from the podium and made my way to my seat. As I walked through the crowd, one by one people stood and applauded, until everyone in the room was on their feet and clapping.

When I reached my seat, a gentleman standing at the back of the room put his hand in the air: a request to speak.

Everyone sat down as the man began to recount how he had been a Lions member during my time at the ranch. He told them he remembered the days of bear crawls and carrying bricks, and he was the person who got Bert fired for child abuse.

And then I recognized him. It was Gordon Slogatt, and I remembered seeing him at the ranch all those years ago.

Gordon then looked at me and the room grew quiet.

"After we fired Bert," he said, "I wanted to make sure that no boy would ever carry those bricks at the ranch again so I bought every last one of them."

I was speechless and overcome with emotion; I was a grown man now, but it took every bit of my strength to hold back my tears. One of the women officers realized I was too emotional to respond, and kindly made her way to the podium and began closing comments, including thanking me for coming and speaking to them.

"I am inspired by your story," she said.

*****

On my way out, Gordon stopped me and said he had something to show me. He lived just a few blocks away.

"Would you ride with me to my house?" he asked.

The Boy Who Carried Bricks

We got in my car, and I drove down the street and around the corner until we came to a nice home on the corner. We both got out of the car and that's when I saw them: The bricks I had once carried, now a harmless patio and sidewalk in front of his house.

I stood at the edge of the driveway and stared at the bricks that had caused me so much pain. *That's where bricks belong*, I thought to myself. *In a house or a sidewalk or a patio, not in the arms of little boys.*

Finally, I drew enough strength to reach down and touch one of them. They looked just as red and heavy and hard as when I was a boy. But instead of their weight dragging me down, now I was standing on them.

I thanked Gordon and started for my car. That's when I noticed one brick off to the side. Before I could even ask, Gordon told me I could have it.

I thanked Gordon again, and then ran to get the brick. As I carried it to my car I couldn't help thinking that it wasn't nearly as heavy as I remembered it being.

I got in my car and drove off with the brick in my lap. As I rounded the corner, I could no longer hold back the tears. I cried so hard I had to pull over because I could hardly see where I was going.

I sat in my car in that parking lot staring at the brick, reliving in my mind all the times I had carried bricks at the ranch until I was certain I had carried the very brick that was now in my lap.

And then I drove back to Gordon's house.

I rounded the corner and parked in the driveway, got out of my car, and started counting the bricks in the front patio. Then I counted the ones in the brick sidewalk and every other brick on Gordon's property. I counted them one by one knowing I had not only touched, but carried them all.

And then I went home to my family.

About the Author

A former police officer, Alton Carter is director of youth ministries for the First United Methodist Church of Stillwater, Oklahoma, and a graduate of Oklahoma State University. The father of two sons—Kelton and Colin, he loves spending time with his family, working with youngsters, and fishing. He makes his home in Stillwater, with his wife, Kristin, and his boys. This is his first book. Visit him at www.AltonCarter.net.

Inspire

In the hopes of being able to assist foster children pursue their dreams of attending college, a portion of the proceeds from this book will go to the Inspire Foundation, which was started by the author to assist young adults where the system leaves off. You can learn more about his foundation work at www.AltonCarterInspireFoundation.com.